Foreword
by Mark Schwarzer OAM

Goalkeeping is a dog-eat-dog world. Each of us survives as best they can, knowing that one day we might be painted as the hero and the very next the villain. A save is just as important as a goal, but rarely does a save draw the same amount of praise. We are literally the only line of defence in football that comprises a single player. Alone with our responsibility – and with our thoughts – we are suspended on the uneasy edge between inaction and intervention for 90 long minutes.

Those 90 minutes are just as long if you're a goalkeeper who is not playing. Bum warming the bench, maybe resenting the person who was picked ahead of you, or resolving to train harder and be better.

It's no wonder people think we're a crazy bunch. We are a special breed, I'll give you that. And for sure, some goalkeepers are arrogant, using their ego as a barrier to protect themselves from the inevitable post-match finger-pointing. But I don't think that's a necessary characteristic.

I was quite sensitive, especially when I was younger, and that made me desperate for encouragement. Back in the nineties and early 2000s that was not a good way to be, because vulnerability was seen as a weakness. At the very least, it was awkward for men to talk about.

What I really needed was for someone more senior to pull me aside and ask how I was going – just take the time to offer some feedback or reassurance. That never really came, and I spent most of my professional career in a heightened state, playing in constant fear that any mistake would be my last. I was caught in this no-man's-land where I had to perform to stay in the team, but performing at my very best was a struggle because I had that fear in the back of my mind.

These are traits I did not recognise in Mackenzie Arnold the first time I watched her play, for the Matildas in a 2018 friendly against England. I liked what I saw at London's Craven Cottage; Mackenzie had an impressive presence in goal and dominated her 18-yard box. However, as the pages of this book attest, the external confidence I witnessed from the stands that night belied some internal sensitivities and insecurities not dissimilar to the ones I had experienced during my playing days.

I would not learn this first-hand for another three years, when Mackenzie and I spoke for the first time. It was in 2021 that her older brother Sam reached out through Facebook. He offered some context around the challenges she had been facing, particularly with the national team and her place in it. Having been initially overlooked for Australia's Tokyo Olympics squad, she ended up travelling

MACCA

Emma Kemp is a sports journalist with the *Sydney Morning Herald* who grew up in Kiama, moved to Sydney and then London, and now lives in Bowral. She has covered numerous FIFA Women's and Men's World Cups, Olympics and Commonwealth Games, and has been fortunate enough to witness from relatively close quarters the Matildas' explosion in popularity that culminated in their historic run to the 2023 World Cup semi-finals. Emma studied journalism at the University of Technology in Sydney and has a Master in International Relations from UNSW. When she grows up she would like to become a firefighter.

MACCA

MY STORY SO FAR

MACKENZIE ARNOLD

with EMMA KEMP

PENGUIN BOOKS

UK | USA | Canada | Ireland | Australia
India | New Zealand | South Africa | China

Penguin Books is part of the Penguin Random House group of companies,
whose addresses can be found at global.penguinrandomhouse.com.

Penguin
Random House
Australia

First published by Penguin Books, 2024

Cover design by Alex Ross © Penguin Random House Australia Pty Ltd
Front cover image: Stephen McCarthy/Getty Images
Back cover image: Brendon Thorne/Getty Images
Typeset in Sabon by Midland Typesetters, Australia

Printed and bound in Australia by Griffin Press, an accredited
ISO AS/NZS 14001 Environmental Management Systems printer

A catalogue record for this
book is available from the
NATIONAL LIBRARY OF AUSTRALIA   National Library of Australia

ISBN 978 1 76134 734 4

penguin.com.au

MIX
Paper | Supporting
responsible forestry
FSC® C018684

*We at Penguin Random House Australia acknowledge that Aboriginal and Torres
Strait Islander peoples are the Traditional Custodians and the first storytellers of the
lands on which we live and work. We honour Aboriginal and Torres Strait Islander
peoples' continuous connection to Country, waters, skies and communities.
We celebrate Aboriginal and Torres Strait Islander stories, traditions and
living cultures; and we pay our respects to Elders past and present.*

Contents

to Japan after all, as one of the extra injury and illness replacements permitted because of the COVID-19 pandemic, but ended up watching the entire tournament from the stands. She returned feeling disenchanted.

Sam hoped that, given I live in the UK, where Mackenzie played her club football for West Ham, I might be able to contact her and offer some support and encouragement. I did, and we communicated back and forth a bit via text messages. She shared some of her frustrations, and I noticed how hard she was on herself. At one point I suggested she use each setback as motivation to prove people wrong. Mostly, though, we just talked.

I had no idea the exchange would have any kind of lasting influence until after the 2023 World Cup, when Mackenzie brought it up during a media interview. I couldn't for the life of me remember what I had said that had apparently been so profound. She explained to me that it wasn't a particular phrase or quote that stuck with her, rather the simple fact that she had felt acknowledged and worth somebody else's time.

This answer, and everything that occurred in those intervening two years, says a lot about where Mackenzie's self-belief was then and where it is now. I am humbled and honoured to think I may have played a small part in that growth, but I also know that 99 per cent of it came from her. You can get all the advice in the world, meet all the people and see all the things, but how you process that – and whether you ultimately do what you need to do to help yourself – has to come from within.

That said, I can also see the invaluable imprint of Tony Franken. The Matildas' goalkeeping coach since 2021, he has guided Mackenzie and her fellow goalkeepers with the same quiet authority he showed in our own coach–player relationship within the Socceroos set-up. Tony's experience in the game – across four men's World Cups – is peerless. He is good at giving instructions and communicating technical information, but he also cares deeply about his goalkeepers' development as both players and people – a rare quality I did not find in many other goalkeeping coaches throughout my European club career.

The quality of goalkeeping across the global women's game has improved out of sight. The difference even between the 2019 and 2023 World Cups was stark, and completely new player pathways have opened up. These developments are in line with the overall growth of women's football, and Australia was lucky enough to observe the full picture from close quarters during the Matildas' historic run to the semi-final.

These external factors have undoubtedly helped to drive Mackenzie's goalkeeping craft to a new level. In the end, though, the buck stops with the individual. All the credit belongs to her. Her achievements are the product of her own resilience and self-belief. They are her biggest assets, and something us goalkeepers need in spades. There is no hiding in goal. Oftentimes, the criticism comes thicker and faster than the praise. Only other goalkeepers fully understand how alone a goalkeeper can feel within a team.

I watched closely during the first half of 2023 as Mackenzie established herself as the Matildas' first-choice keeper, and then throughout the tournament as the resilience and self-belief she had built was tested and then ultimately reinforced. When her performance did not meet her own high standards – such as Australia's group-stage loss to Nigeria – she took a good look at what had gone wrong and moved forward, armed with insight and experience. She did not put a foot wrong before or after that game – and that is even before considering her role in the famous penalty shootout against France.

Through my TV work, I was fortunate enough to be pitchside at Suncorp Stadium on the night of 12 August 2023. I remain in disbelief at what I witnessed. To save three penalties in a World Cup quarter-final shootout is remarkable in itself. To have made the third save after having taken – and missed – her own spot kick, which would have been the winner, is extraordinary. But there it was: the strength of mind and nerves of steel to set aside what might have been and focus on securing another chance.

When she did, and the Matildas progressed to the semi-final and wrote themselves into Australian sporting folklore, I said live on air that this would go down as the biggest performance of any Australian goalkeeper in history. I stand by that statement. Yes, I have been a part of some pretty intense penalty shootouts, including quite a well-known one against Uruguay back in 2005, but this was something else. This was Mackenzie Arnold in 2023.

Prologue

Penalties. Two teams can play football for a full 120 minutes, for a combined 36 shots on goal, 20 corners and 841 passes, only for the whole thing to be rendered irrelevant as soon as the full-time whistle goes. Then everything comes down to an entirely different kind of contest.

That's the case at the end of extra time in the World Cup quarter-final, on home soil, against France. The game has become an exaggeration of actual football. Hearts and careers are both broken and mended by penalty shootouts, and I'm a tragic from way back. Having said that, the anticipation can be a bit scary.

I can already see it in the middle distance when, in the 107th minute, I stick up a left glove to stop Vicki Bècho scoring the first goal of the game. That would be worse, I decide in an instant, than losing a World Cup quarter-final on penalties. Direct culpability and all that. Two minutes later, Grace Geyoro whips in a cross that requires another intervention at my near post before Steph Catley cleans up the rest. In the ruckus, Alanna Kennedy is down after a head clash with Eugénie Le Sommer and needs a head-injury assessment before she can return to play. I don't even hear the outnumbered French support trying in vain to take over Suncorp Stadium. Don't they know this is the most Aussie ground ever? I know – I've been sitting in those stands since I was a toddler. But this is not the thing responsible for my racing mind as I deny Bècho once more late in the second half of extra time. I am picturing the shootout saves I might make and the consequences of a win or a loss. For me. For the Matildas. For women's football. I am thinking too deeply. What's the deal with that? And why are France subbing on a back-up goalkeeper? Solène Durand has made just two senior international appearances and both came in friendlies. Is she especially good at saving penalties? Can someone wearing green and gold not just score in the next 30 seconds?

There's the whistle. The saving grace. The signal that it is time to actually *do* the shootout rather than angst over it while the other team are still throwing the kitchen sink my way. I am in game mode. Right now, I don't want inspirational talks. I just need to get to our goalkeeper coach, Tony Franken, so we can finalise our plan. But Tony is talking at 100 miles an hour, running through analyses of all the different kickers. I'm feeling good but the wave of information has the potential to overwhelm me. 'Tony, stop, it's too much,' I say. 'We'll take it as it comes.' He understands instantly, stops talking, and that is that. I'm only half-listening to the team huddle behind me.

The appointment and order of our penalty takers has nothing to do with me. That is, until I hear the voice of our manager, Tony Gustavsson: 'Macca.' I turn around to see Tony G. holding up five fingers. I know what that means even before he says, 'You will take the fifth penalty.'

This is the same coach who, two years earlier, had told me I'd played my way out of the Tokyo Olympics team. Whose supposed lack of faith had made me so angry I wanted to leave the Matildas for good. Maybe even leave West Ham. Go home to Queensland. Play AFLW, perhaps. Do literally anything except keep trying to make it in an environment that had slowly consumed every scrap of my confidence.

At that point, in mid-2021, I had been called up to the national team for a total of 96 matches since my debut in 2012, but had only played 26 times. The discrepancy between these two numbers has long been the central thread of my compromised self-worth. Each reminder of this, especially in recent years, constituted a fresh little stab in the guts that sapped just a little bit more sense of belonging. By the time my Olympics omission rolled around, I was drained.

Ninety-six and 26. The first number represented more than a decade of experience in the Matildas set-up. It denoted all the friends I'd made and the family we had created. The second was a marker of separation. That came first in the physical form. Like when those friends with all those extra caps had seats in the front of the plane and I was sitting further back because I had next to none (a completely fair system, in my view). And like the mornings after games, when most of the girls I hung out with were taken for a recovery session while I went to regular training because I hadn't played.

Then there was the mental disconnect. Brought on when some coaches questioned my attitude and my friendships, asking if I should be hanging out with first XI regulars when I was not a starter myself. Players such as Alanna, Caitlin Foord and Sam Kerr have been my best mates since we were kids – but these kinds of interrogations still left me feeling unsure of how to act while in camp. Joking around in the changerooms was frowned upon because I wasn't backing it up on the pitch. I was once told it was okay for Sam to have a laugh because she was Sam Kerr. The intimation was that she would almost certainly do something incredible during the next game. If I was caught mucking around, though, I had no way of balancing that with on-field performance. How do you prove yourself from the bench?

In many ways, my struggle to become a regular starter for Australia was simply a part of the goalkeeper's curse. Where outfield players are regularly subbed on mid-match, back-up shot-stoppers are rarely called upon – usually only when the goalkeeper already out there gets injured. Goalkeepers can spend their entire careers not playing, even at club level. My club form was almost always solid; I just could not seem to translate the way I played for West Ham into my time with the national team. On the rare occasions I was given a chance, I felt as if I had been set up to fail. I now understand that was largely down to my own mindset.

In retrospect, I used to take a lot of football decisions personally. My Olympics non-selection, for example, had nothing to do with my worth as a person. But my brain, at the time, took the rejection and used it to confirm all the negative thoughts swirling around in there. The insecurities were endless. If I saw Tony G. having a joke with another player, it meant he felt more comfortable in their presence than he did in mine. A meeting with another player meant he cared more about her than me. Working with another individual during a training session meant he had more time to help her game than he did mine. For so long, I sought external validation to counter my lack of self-belief. The irony was that, even when others attempted to provide me with the assurance I craved, I did not know how to accept it.

No one tells you how segregated you can feel from your team's successes or failures when you are not actively contributing. While it was technically my third World Cup, I had not played a minute of World Cup football before the 2023 tournament. I was given one match at the Rio Olympics in 2016 – the 'easy' group game against Zimbabwe – and spent Tokyo 2020 watching from the stands.

I had decided to go to Japan, initially as a travelling reserve, following a swift intervention from Alanna in a hotel lobby. A day after that, when the International Olympic Committee announced it would allow each nation to select an additional four players on top of the regular

18 to cater for the complications caused by COVID-19, Tony G. told me I was back in. I was still furious, and made it clear I was not going for him but for my teammates. He told me he accepted that, that he understood. I never even made it onto the bench.

How can you say that you have grown as a person when you are averse to speaking positively about yourself? For me, maybe the best way to explain it is that, at some point towards the end of 2022, I started to care less about things outside of my control. I am still an overthinker – it takes longer than nine months to undo a decade of self-sabotage, and I have much further to go. Yet I am now able to process experiences and interactions in a healthier way. I guess I feel more mature. My coaches would probably call this professionalism. The capacity to accept football decisions for what they are, to take your opportunities and learn from your mistakes.

Now here he is, Tony G. the coach (different from Tony G. the person), telling me I will take the fifth penalty. Watching as my eyes widen and checking once more whether this is okay. All the girls are looking at me. I am so caught up in my own shock I cannot assess the level of theirs. I know there are two possible paths to start down at this point: the one that involves feeling a lot of stress and the other that demands I release the tension, accept the task I have been given and get on with it. France win the coin toss and will take the first kick.

As I walk towards the goal, the sound of 50,000 people threatens to turn my composure to mush. It's almost deafening, even though I am not wearing my hearing aids. The roar is zealous support laced with tension – fans with a huge investment in the outcome. An outcome that depends on me. In sport, a lot of talk centres around the pressure of the occasion. How it feels for different athletes – whether they overcome it or channel it to their advantage. Sometimes there are details about their internal dialogue or external sensory signals. The truth is, when you are at the epicentre of one of these occasions, you often can't really think at all. Okay, this is not entirely true. Fragments of thought do begin to form but they are buzzy little half-thoughts that flit around next to other half-thoughts and dissolve before you've had a chance to catch them. And why even bother trying, when the only thing you really need to catch is the ball?

I stare at the ground as I walk, my back to the crowd, seeking to block it all out. Feeling my heart beating out of my chest as I shake Durand's hand and wish her luck. The referee, Chilean María Carvajal, warns both of us about keeping at least one foot on the goal line until the ball has left the penalty taker's boot. My eyes stay down, focused on a nondescript spot a little further afield. Thinking. Not thinking. Waiting. Then, I complete my final walk.

The crowd is a low hum now but I can still *feel* it. I can sense every pair of eyes in the place on me and on France's first penalty taker, Selma Bacha. Once I have taken my place in goal, it's just her and me. Beyond the 12 yards separating us, nobody else exists. Bacha seems nervous. She does not look up at me once, instead shifting her gaze from her feet to the ball and back again. Goalkeepers are trained to pick up on these little clues. Part of the position is understanding the inner workings of a kicker's mind. Are they anxious? Are they confident? Are they looking in one direction or the other? Are they doing that because they will actually go that way or are they doing it to trick me? I generally don't move around a lot while they are preparing, mainly because it distracts me from figuring out what my opponent is thinking.

A confident kicker often loves these kinds of mind games; the others just want to get it over with. I can already tell Bacha is in the latter camp. I bounce on the spot, my knees slightly bent, weight balanced on the balls of my feet. To the naked eye, this stance appears neutral, border-line harmless, but from here I can launch myself to cover any part of the goal. I know this. Bacha knows this. We both also know that, because she is the taker, the odds are stacked in her favour. She *should* score. That concept alone can be enough to psych some players out. And as I watch her flickering eyes, I think I can *just* see her observing me, searching for micro-movements that might give something up. I have a hunch she is going to wait for me to budge first before deciding which way she'll go – and I know instantly that this means I am going to revert to my original tech-nique. I also know that Tony Franken will not necessarily approve, because he spent the lead-up to this tournament teaching me a new technique.

Using my technique, as the taker approached the ball I would try to make her second-guess her direction and sometimes look to even change her mind mid-action. On the flip side, timing is everything. If I make that move a split-second too early, I may be exposed before they have released the ball. If I do it too late, I can't manoeuvre my body quickly enough in the other direction to cover enough goal to save the ball. Tony F. understandably had reservations about these margins for error and worked with me on another technique. His technique ensured I could cover as much goal as possible on whichever side I chose. It is no surprise this is the most common technique used for penalties.

It was a technique we would continue to work on after each training session just before the World Cup. We were in what we call pre-camp on the Gold Coast and the girls were practising penalties. Teammates have always told me penalty shootouts are my specialty. I have saved quite a few over the years. A few said my technique made me the hardest keeper to practise against. On this particular day in pre-camp, however, I did not save a single one. Every member of the squad had a crack and every member of the squad scored. I just couldn't get the hang of it. Either I chose the wrong way or I chose correctly but failed to get enough power behind me to reach the ball. The more I floundered, the more visibly frustrated I became, to the point that a few of the girls noticed and came to ask me if I was okay. I hadn't informed any of them about the modification I was learning but Caitlin saw it. She marched up to me and asked me point blank: 'Why did you change your technique?' I wasn't ready to remove what felt most natural. Not until I had perfected what Tony F. was trying to teach me. I resolved to use both depending on the situation.

Caitlin's voice is in my head now as I stare Bacha down, reminding me to play to my strengths. And I have a gut feeling. So, as she begins her run-up, I dive to my right. My body knows before it hits the turf that I have covered enough territory – part conscious thought, part muscle memory. Push off with my right foot, close down the angle, make the save.

I notice a lack of power in her shot. Does that mean she changed her mind based on her belief I would dive to my left? Who knows, but I will take this version of events to my deathbed. I get up as quickly as I've gone down and holler, 'Come on.' Ellie Carpenter – a club teammate of Bacha's at Lyon – is going absolutely bananas. I live for Ellie's celebrations. I especially live for them when I have just saved the first penalty in a World Cup quarter-final. Then, my face returns to steel and I take my leave.

As Durand takes up her position in goal, Caitlin leaves our huddle at the halfway line and walks to the spot. I am a massive rugby league fan and it gives me such pleasure watching Cait set up for a pen at Suncorp. Once she has positioned the ball, she takes four steps back and then two to the left, as if she is readying for a conversion. After a stuttered run-up, she sneaks a powerful spot kick into the side netting. Probably not the way Durand imagined making her international competitive debut. Australia lead 1–0. The stands sound like thunder.

My turn again. This time, it's Kadidiatou Diani and she is surer of herself than Bacha. She has four goals and three assists so far this tournament – nobody has been involved in more goals. I commit and step out to my right prematurely. As soon as I realise I've gone too early, I try to compensate for it by moving back the other way. In the end, the only mind games I played were with myself. Diani approaches the ball as if she is going to leather it and then coolly slots it past my right side. All I had to do was follow through with the initial motion. This annoys me immensely. Bloody hell, why didn't I just make my decision and stick with it? 1–1.

Steph Catley's attempt is saved by Durand. I notice Durand is taking her time walking to the goal for Australia's penalties, making our takers wait. This is a common mind game in shootouts. But I am impatient to keep the momentum going and am straight back out there to wait for Wendie Renard. A tall centre-back, standing at 1.87 metres. The Lyon captain. The French captain. An icon in her country with all the confidence in the world. I try to read her and fail, so I stick with what we had pre-planned for her: dive to my left. Wrong way. Renard buries her penalty to my right, the direction that all five thus far have gone. Advantage France, 2–1.

The pressure is on Sam now. She must score the next penalty to keep the scores level. I know she will be thinking about the pen she missed at the 2019 World Cup, in the round-of-16 loss to Norway. She went high and wide that time, which was not how she usually went about it.

This would be a return to the routine. Again, Durand takes her time walking out but it has no effect on Sam. Her calf injury stopped her from playing any part in the group stage and it's been so good having her back in the knock-out rounds. This place exploded when she came off the bench during regular time. Even that feels an age ago. The whole match is already a blur. Clarity only comes if I make my focus very small. I am here to save penalties. Just like at training. Sam is ice cold. She opts for low and to the keeper's left. Durand leaves it too late. 2–2.

I now face Eugénie Le Sommer, knowing her vibe will be similar to that of Renard. We had managed to keep France's record goalscorer out for 120 minutes. Now it's one on one and she knows exactly what she is doing. Her nose is swollen and bloodied from her head clash with Alanna. Her eyes are unmoving. I take a half-step to my left before diving to my right. This time, it probably would not have mattered what I did. Le Sommer had already picked my left side as her target and succeeded thanks to a tricky run-up, careering forward as if about to pound the ball with all her might and then delicately passing it into the opposite corner. France lead 3–2.

As soon as I see Mary Fowler, it's clear she will have no problem. An old soul for a 20-year-old, Mary strides up as if she's at training with nobody watching. Sets up as if the eyes of 50,000 people are not boring into her and runs into her spot kick with such natural ability she has signalled it is in the net before it even is. 3–3. I can see France's huddle shifting nervously.

I knew before the match that the fifth penalty would be the one to save. Now I am remembering what I do not want to remember: my turn is next. If I do save this one, I can then score and win it for us. If I don't save and then I miss, our World Cup will be over. Dread creeps up my throat. I force it back down and concentrate on Ève Périsset. A defender. Sam's teammate at Chelsea. That is the extent of my education. In times like this, trying too hard can backfire. In times like this, you just have to trust your coach's planning – might as well throw everything at it and see what happens.

I hurl myself on a 45-degree angle to my right. It closes the distance but the ball is still tracking on a wider trajectory. I will my right arm to stretch, order every fibre of my being to soften and give me just a little more reach. Then I feel it, brushing the fingertips of my glove. The contact is so light – but enough to alter the flight path. I am big enough to admit there is no way I would have reached that without Tony F.'s method. I feel so grateful for him right now. He has always had my back and he knows exactly what I need to perform. I respond best to a mixture of encouragement and tough love, and he treads that fine line so flawlessly I can't help but want to work hard for him. Behind me, the sound of synthetic leather on wood is unmistakable. I swing around to check the ball is not about to roll in off the post. The joy I feel at seeing it ricochet well out of reach lasts approximately two seconds before reality sets in. My time has come. France have taken their first five penalties. We have taken only four. The score is tied at 3–3 and best-of-five rules stipulate that I need only convert our fifth penalty to seal our place in the semi-finals. It would be the first time an Australian football team – male or female – has made it to the final four of a World Cup.

I retrieve the ball and walk to the spot. It is difficult to explain what my heart is doing. Pounding so hard it might burst through my chest. Not beating fast, though, but big and heavy. I try to breathe through it, search for something to bring my vital signs down a notch. That does not work. Nothing will help me in this moment. I have practised this penalty a few times. One thing is certain and one thing is not. I always go the same way – to my right – and I don't always hit it very well. When I do find the sweet spot, though, I'm positive no keeper can stop it. I set the ball down then set myself up. Seven steps in total. Eyes down. Eyes up. Durand is primed in her goal. Waiting for me to score. Waiting for me to miss. I take a deep breath, then one more, and then I go for it.

The width of a goalpost is 12 centimetres. For a goalkeeper, that can be the difference between conceding or not. Between keeping a clean sheet or not. My role dictates that, broadly speaking, I naturally like it much better if a ball hits at an angle that ensures it bounces back out and not in. It is unusual to find myself hoping for the opposite. When my penalty leaves my boot, I know I've hit it nicely. When it flies in the direction of the top corner, I feel sure it is going in. In the milliseconds after hearing the awful sound of it clattering into the post, I hope the angle has been kind. It has not. The rebound occurs with such force that the ball is almost back at the halfway line before my hands have moved to my head and my head has turned to face my teammates. They look as ruined as I feel. We were so close. The air is sucked out of the stadium. Everything is deathly quiet.

1.

First Steps

I reckon I'd be a good subject for a nature-versus-nurture study, because when I was born on 25 February 1994, at Allamanda Private Hospital on the Gold Coast, I feel sure I popped out with a rugby league gene. I suppose there is also the possibility that I was a Queenslander through and through before I could even talk. Then, there were environmental factors, such as my father and brother, Sam, who watched rugby league religiously and let me watch with them. It was all I knew. No other sport existed. Not even soccer. I was going to be Brisbane's next fullback. Never mind that women didn't play much league in the 1990s. Boring details like that weren't going to stop me from becoming the next Lockyer. Neither was the fact Mum refused to sign me up. My fledgling league dream would have to be kept alive and thriving on our family's front lawn.

Sam was five and a half years older than me and had played a bit on an actual field growing up but his significant hearing loss meant he had to stop as soon as the kids got old enough to start playing rough and head knocks became a risk. His little sister and a front yard in Robina were the next best thing. Our yard wasn't big, maybe about eight metres – just enough to get in two or three tackles. And the try line was the cut-off between the grass and the concrete of our driveway, which meant a lot of grazes from stretching or diving to ground the ball on the concrete. We played against each other but switched to the same team whenever an errant ball needed quick retrieval before it escaped onto the road and down the massive hill that took ages to run down and back up. When we weren't doing that, we were tackling each other on the trampoline and riding our scooters and skateboards.

But league was the constant. When I became old enough to understand, Dad told me about Wally Lewis and some other greats of the game. In those early days, though, I only had eyes for Lockyer. Posters covered my bedroom wall. Of him in his Broncos kit and him in his Maroons kit. We went to games at Suncorp Stadium as a family and I was transfixed by his ability to single-handedly change a game – a skill he carried through his transition to becoming a five-eighth.

My most formative NRL memory is Brisbane's 15–8 premiership-winning grand final of 2006. We had some family friends over and they had kids my age. In my mind, this gathering made me a cool 12-year-old who threw a 'party' to watch the footy. Some of us supported Melbourne Storm and some of us the Broncos, so I made a massive sign that read 'Honk for Broncos'. We went out to the main street, out the front of the house, and held it up to try and prompt some hearty honks as our fellow citizens drove past. It's one of those core memories that makes me laugh out loud every time I think about it.

Another is a Broncos home game against St George Illawarra. I couldn't tell you what year but I do know that Suncorp was sold out and my entire family was present – even my nana, who was visiting from Wollongong. It was a pretty special time with the whole crew there. We jumped on the train at Nerang, riding it all the way to the stadium. Me, decked out head to toe in Broncos gear, carrying my flag and my big blow-up finger. It was all very exciting. Half-time was a trip to the concourse to buy hot chips and a drink – I got a bottle of Fanta. Soon after the restart, it was gone. I had momentarily put it down to rest in between my legs – without putting the lid on. When Brisbane scored a try seconds later, I jumped to my feet to cheer and wave my flag. I didn't realise that the fizzy orange liquid had spilled all over the man sitting directly in front of me. It soaked his jacket through. My brother was quick to grab the bottle and apologise but the man certainly wasn't happy.

Even now, living in London, I get up in the mornings to watch Brisbane play from afar. I get through as much of the game as I can before training – my partner Kirsty will drive and I'll have the first half playing on my phone and then in the breakfast room. The second half often clashes with our session so I make sure I stay off social media until I can get back home and watch the rest of the game on replay.

STEVE ARNOLD, father

When Kenz was about 10 or 11, she tackled me flat on my back. I was coming out of my and Leah's bedroom – when I looked up, she was charging down the hallway. Before I knew it, she had me around the waist, picked me up and drove me down onto the bed. I weigh about 90 kilos and she lifted me clean off my feet. Straight away, I heard the base beneath the mattress crack and the next morning we had to go out and buy another bed frame. She thought it was pretty funny.

I lived for Friday night footy and was the adjudicator of our family tipping competition. At the start of every NRL season, I crafted these little boxes out of paper. One for me, one for Dad and one for Sam. I wrote one of our names on each box. Then I prepared the tips on another piece of paper, listing all the fixtures along with who each of us was backing. The winner of each round received a $1 coin, retrieved from the piggy bank in the kitchen and deposited into their paper box. If I couldn't find a dollar in the piggy bank, I usually went to Mum and asked her for one. The person with the most dollars in their box at the end of the season won and got to keep the money. Sam and Dad thought the whole thing was a bit silly; I obviously thought it was genius. There was a side hustle for me, too. As the tipping overlord, I was in control of the cash and the only person who paid much attention to exactly how many dollars were in circulation at any given point in time. It meant nobody else knew if a couple went missing here and there.

Sam and I didn't really get pocket money as kids. Not that we ever felt skint – if I went to the movies or out somewhere else, Mum and Dad would slip me $10. On top of that, we could also save up our Christmas and birthday money to spend on whatever we pleased. So we didn't really need pocket money and there was no incentivised chores-for-cash system. We just did jobs around the house when asked. Before dinner, Mum often called us to set the table and unpack the dishwasher, and we always had to clean our rooms and make our beds. Mum was a bit of a clean freak – everything had to be just so. I always found it nonsensical that we had to clean our room before the cleaner came. I would say to Mum, 'But the cleaner's coming.' And she'd say, 'But I'll be embarrassed if the place isn't clean.' I thought that was the whole point of a cleaner, but anyway.

Mum has always been the head of the family, the key decision-maker. When we were young, if we ever asked Dad for something, the response would usually be, 'Ask Mum.' So we'd go to her and she would make the executive decisions. If the opposite ever occurred and she told us to, 'Ask Dad,' we already knew that it would be a yes. I think that was the case for me more than Sam. Dad was a lot harder on my brother than he was on me. It might have been the age gap or that he was a boy, but I have been a daddy's girl since the moment I was born. Every weekend he took me to the shops and every weekend I returned home with a massive cup of pick-and-mix lollies that I would never finish. Of course, Mum would order him to get me a smaller cup next time. And, of course, the following weekend I returned with a cup the same size.

As a family, we have never been overly affectionate with our words or actions but I have never doubted how much we all love each other. Mum is a strong-minded woman who has never been afraid to stand up for both herself and for what she believes in. It's something I've always admired about her and one reason I've tried so hard to make her proud. She can be pretty stubborn, too, and her tough love has definitely hardened my shell as I've grown older. This would be the point when those closest to me would remind me that I am also pretty stubborn. I suppose I know where I get it from. My dad is more chilled out and goes with the flow, and I see a lot of him in me, too. I suppose my personality is a perfect mix of both parents (some might disagree with the perfect part). I've always gone to Mum for her opinion, advice or outlook and gone to Dad when I needed a bit of love.

My brother Sam is my best friend, which is funny given we couldn't stand each other when we were kids. Front-lawn league aside, we fought non-stop, both verbally and physically. Like typical siblings. And also like typical siblings, the younger thought deep down that the older was the coolest person around. I tried to follow Sam and his mates everywhere and copy everything he did, including how he dressed. When I was five or six, he was 11 or 12 and going through that phase of wearing satin boxers under his shorts. I desperately wanted to do it too but knew I would never be allowed, so I operated in secret. One morning, before we were due to go as a family to some mud-boat races in Brisbane, I snuck a pair of my own boxers under the shorts I was wearing. The day in question turned out to be one of summer's hottest and anybody who has ever worn satin anything will know it is not the most breathable material. I wanted to get these boxers off so badly but was terrified of getting into trouble with Mum for having them on in the first place. So I said nothing and sat in my sweat. Hours later, it got too much and I confessed. To my great relief, she thought it was very amusing.

We moved to Mermaid Waters when I was about nine. Our home was near one of the canals and Sam got a tinnie for his birthday. He and his friends used to love that tinnie and went out fishing all the time. Whenever my friends and I knew he and his mates were about to use it, we'd race down and take it out to the middle of the canal and just sit there. He could see us from the deck and would holler for us to come back, and we would then pretend the motor wouldn't start.

SAM ARNOLD, brother

Kenz was a massive tomboy and I believe that's largely because she tagged along to a lot of the stuff I was doing with friends. We were always creating a bit of mischief, terrorising the neighbours by shining laser lights through their windows or putting things in their letter boxes. We would play knock and run and make Mackenzie do the knocking. It was almost like we were setting her up for trouble because we wanted to see a reaction. There was one old neighbour in particular we used to agitate a lot with this sort of thing. We would knock and then rush back into our own house to hide, and he would stride over to our place and knock on the door and let off some steam at Mum. That's the sort of thing Kenz would be hanging around when she was little. Because she was so much smaller than the rest of us, we always sort of protected her and kept a close eye on her. But just by being there, she picked up a lot of words and phrases she probably shouldn't have and became a bit of a smart alec quite young. That informed her witty personality a bit, I think.

She wasn't afraid to play a game of footy and be knocked around. By the middle of her primary school years, she was hanging out with her own friends a lot more. They were mostly all boys from her soccer team. She matched it with them on the field. I think because she was always running around with us, she had a bit of a head-start in her development. The physicality was never too much for her; she got enjoyment out of it. Once she was eight or nine, she was the person up front scoring the goals. It's actually quite mind-blowing how she's gone from that position to a goalkeeper. But her frame wasn't really built for speed and she began to fall behind most other kids. By that point, her advantage was her technical ability with the ball at her feet.

My brother moved out when he was 17. I was about 12 – the age when we were starting to relate to each other a little bit more and could have a normal conversation. It was only after he left and I didn't see him every day that I began to realise how much I loved having him around. I missed him. Over time, we have just got closer and closer, and now I don't know what I'd do without him. Sam has been there for me through everything and I go to him with just about anything. He is also probably the most honest, in a round-about way. Mum is the most direct with her honesty and

Dad is very careful about being honest with me, especially on the topic of football. But Sam is smart with his words. He almost forces me to be honest with myself. It can be annoying sometimes, because I know what he's doing when he's doing it, but he knows how to help me see his point of view without outright saying it.

I never felt any pressure from Mum and Dad to be good at sport. They didn't have any expectations because they're not overly sporty people. Dad grew up in New Zealand and played a bit of rugby union at school but he describes that time as being the skinny boy on a field surrounded by the hulking locals. Mum always said he was so skinny he could run around in the shower and not get wet. But Dad liked watching sport. Mum would probably prefer to watch *Come Dine with Me*. The pair of them were about as clueless as me when it came to what talent looked like and whether I had any. I did what a lot of kids do: gave everything a go. I was in dancing, gymnastics, nippers and tennis. You name it, I tried it. Golf was probably the one my parents pushed the most, because they both enjoyed playing on weekends and Sam was pretty good, too. I wasn't about it. I was just so bored. I even had some lessons for a bit but couldn't pick it up and found it frustrating. I also disliked the solitary element. You are often by yourself and not talking to anyone. There are no teammates. It's just you, standing there, swinging a club. In the end, Mum conceded and let me stop. Sam was good at tennis as well but didn't thrive competitively. During tournaments, you could tell he was deep in his own head, as if playing more against himself than his opponent. That was always one of the downsides of individual sports for me – the lack of camaraderie.

STEVE ARNOLD

She didn't like tennis once she had to start running and chasing the ball, so she wasn't really cut out for that. She definitely liked touch football, though. And I think she could have been pretty good at swimming. She took lessons, as kids do, and it progressed all the way to the coaching stage.

For years, I felt hard done by that I was not going to become the next Lockyer. After a while, though, I started playing soccer with the boys at school. Mum wasn't keen on that because it was a bit too boyish – I doubt I would have ever been signed up if it weren't for my persistence. Playing with the boys at a young age was the best thing to happen to me. Everything was quicker, more intense, more aggressive. It was night and day compared to playing with girls and I had no interest in playing with them. You can tell which women's players started in boys' teams. They just have a bit about them. You have to, or you get eaten alive out there. I remember getting into rumbles and tumbles when I was nine or 10 and getting cheered by the parents when I made a tackle. I guess you could say this is where the competitiveness started to take over.

My first memory of a professional soccer team is the Liverpool jersey my parents bought me during a trip to Melbourne. I have no idea why they chose a Liverpool jersey but, because of that, I decided I would be a Liverpool fan. But then, when I started primary school, one of my classmates went for Newcastle United and suddenly they became my favourite team as well. That's how blasé I was about it – there was a new flavour every week. I can't remember ever watching an English Premier League game.

While my parents didn't push me into sport, once I had chosen to play, they were firm with me. I wasn't allowed to slack off. During my early football days, I also went through a skateboarding phase and I'd often be out the front doing tricks on the gutter. I was told more than once to wear my shoes. One afternoon, soon before we were due to leave for training, I scraped my toe on the concrete and half of my toenail came off. I went inside with blood all over my toe and it hurt too much to fit into my boot. The response was basically that I was going to stop complaining, put my boots on and go to training. I was never allowed to take the easy way out of anything. And if I was told not to do something and I did it anyway, there were consequences – it was my problem to fix.

SAM ARNOLD

Mum wasn't the emotional type during our childhoods. If you fell over and hurt yourself, she wouldn't say, 'Are you okay? Give me a look,' and that sort of thing. She'd be more like, 'You're all right. Give it a rub.' When you put that in the context of Mackenzie's soccer, there was this underlying expectation that kept her on her toes a lot. Kenz had a real mischievous streak growing up, and a tendency to switch off and muck around with friends. If there were games in which she didn't play well – especially if she was messing around – Mum would bring it up. We'd be in the car on the way home and Mum would say things like, 'I'm not going to waste my Saturday doing all this if you are just going to mess around and not be interested.' When Kenz started making those regional teams that required parents to travel more, it just further raised the stakes in Mum's head and gave her more ammunition to work with. Kenz's main concern at that age was being able to play with her friends, so any threat that that could be taken away would make her more focused. Mum is tough as nails and always driving into your head this element of doubt to keep you moving. And I think that kept Kenz on the straight and narrow.

That approach has helped me right up until today – I very rarely pull out of training. It has been drilled into me that I will get through whatever I need to get through. You see some kids now who stop training straight away, if the tiniest thing hurts, and I'm really glad I'm not wired like that.

In 2005, when I was 11, I trialled as a defender for the Gold Coast rep side. I was still happily playing with the Burleigh Heads Bulldogs and had never even considered anything beyond that. But one of the other club mums, whose daughter was also in a boys' team but an older age group, told my mum about the reps. A lot of the other girls trying out had been in the team previously and went to the same school as me, so it felt like I should too. It was an open tryout down at Carrara Stadium, over two or three weeknights a week for about two or three weeks in winter. This was as much an occasion for the parents, who gathered in the dark on camping chairs with drinks in their hands and plenty to catch up on. It was their time to socialise and ours to burn off energy. The coaches put us through our paces and then we all mucked around together afterwards. One event was an informal shooting drill. For some reason, there was no goalkeeper on this particular day, so we all took turns in goal to face shots. Nobody even wore gloves. You just went in for a bit and then someone else took over. Most of us took our shots with the power that one might expect from an 11-year-old girl. But there was this one girl who could smack the ball much harder than all the others. Her name was Tiffany. She was a short, stocky girl with curly blonde hair and seemed to relish absolutely leathering the ball. Nobody was willing to be the obstacle standing between Tiffany and her target. I'm not sure if I had a point to prove or just liked a challenge, but I wasn't that fazed. So I walked into the goal and waited. She took her run-up and, as the ball left her boot and hissed towards me, I just sort of moved my body in front of it. I wouldn't say I stopped it with good technique, but I did stop it. The others were kind of astonished and there were a couple of comments but we were just mucking around.

It wasn't until the last day of trials that it became apparent one of the coaches must have been observing. She approached Mum and I and broke the news that I wasn't going to be selected as a full-back. That didn't really surprise me – I wasn't that great on the field. But then she said they needed a goalkeeper and wanted me in that position. She asked me if I was a goalkeeper. I answered that

I absolutely was not a goalkeeper and it was never going to happen. I had played in the outfield since I was seven and that was fun. I didn't view soccer as anything more than a source of fun, so wasn't going to waste that time trying to do something completely foreign to me.

I was still playing in the outfield with the boys at Robina but, after joining the open women's team as a goalkeeper, I started to warm to the concept. I was exposed to a bit of coaching with the other keepers and, to my surprise, actually started to enjoy it. It felt similar to rugby league, in that someone kicked a ball at me and I had to catch it with my hands. And if I wasn't allowed to play league, this was maybe the next best thing.

PAUL JACKSON, coach

I was coaching the Southport women's team when, after a rep tournament, I was approached by Mackenzie's mother, Leah, to ask if I could recommend a goalkeeper coach. I informed her that I was actually a keeper coach, and offered to have a look at Kenz. We arranged to meet them at the Emmanuel College sports fields, where I could assess Kenz and determine what, if any, skills she possessed and which aspects of her game needed attention. Off the bat, she clearly had the ability and keenness to become a very decent keeper. One thing that stood out was she wasn't afraid to dive – something junior keepers do not usually like doing – and she got the basics correct right from the start. After a year of coaching her, it wasn't hard to see Kenz had a special talent. Her skill level was well above others of her age. I told Leah and anyone else who would listen that she would one day play for the Matildas.

The main problem that needed addressing was the standard of football on the Gold Coast. It wasn't overly strong and I believed she needed to be playing with and against stronger players to develop the game side of her skill set. Kenz had the technique and drive; she just needed to be pushed in a harder environment where she would face more shots and have more touches of the ball. I felt she could get this in Brisbane and called Mike Mulvey. Mike was then coaching Brisbane Roar's A-League and W-League teams, and was director of football at the Queensland Academy of Sports (QAS). I hoped he might be a gateway to the people who really needed to see her. I told him about Kenz and said I was absolutely certain that she needed to be assessed. Mike said he couldn't just accept a player solely on a third-party recommendation, so he invited Kenz and Leah up to the QAS so he could have a look for himself. The three of us drove up together and a day later he called to ask if she could reattend so that the QAS goalkeeper coach Fernando Álvez could assess her. They did so and she was accepted. She was subsequently also invited to train with the Roar women's team.

I did have some reservations. The QAS squad already had two or three keepers, including Casey Dumont, and breaking in would be tough. And over the next few months, I made a few phone calls to express a small area of concern with the programme. Because the squad had a number of goalkeepers, Kenz wasn't getting game time. I spoke with the coaches and asked for special dispensation so she could train with the QAS but play for Southport, the Gold Coast Women's Premier League team. I also asked Southport to allow a non-training player to be in the squad to enable Kenz to maintain her match practice. I agreed not to coach her, as she remained under the QAS keeper coach's jurisdiction. That year, she was voted player of the league.

Her strengths

Shot-stopping: During the initial training that we did at Emmanuel, Kenz was very strong on the basics of footwork and handling, and wasn't afraid to engage in a collapse dive or a full, clear dive. She was very eager to learn and soaked up advice like a sponge.

Distribution: The modern game requires a keeper to be totally proficient in the art of distribution and Kenz was completely at ease with her ability to control the ball and play out from the back in order to maintain possession. She is strong with both feet and has the game awareness to set up attacks all the way from the back by smart use of her distribution skills.

Communication: This is the hardest aspect for a coach to teach. Communicating with your defenders and team is so crucial to the team's ability to play. It also keeps the players in front of the keeper feeling confident. Most young players do not talk at all during a game but it really is a must for a top-level goalkeeper. Kenz's communication was excellent. She delivered instructions to her defenders to help give them a more complete picture of what was happening around them. These were short phrases like 'on your left shoulder', 'show her the line', 'drop off' or 'push up'.

Paul Jackson was essentially my first ever goalkeeper coach. He taught me how to catch and dive properly, all the basics. My parents set up one-on-one coaching sessions with him, on top of whoever else I was training and trialling with at the time. Paul was very soft, very caring. He has dad vibes. But he wasn't a pushover. He was also very knowledgeable. If he needed to tell you that you weren't doing something correctly, he would. He just had a quiet authority about him. I was just a kid, a nobody – not even an established goalkeeper – but he had so much time for me. He helped me get ready to try to get into the QAS and used his connections to set up a trial.

I got in when I was 16 and had to train in Brisbane almost every afternoon. Mum picked me up from school with a packed lunch, drove me an hour and a bit to Brisbane, sat for an hour or two while I trained and then drove us for another hour and a bit back home. We would get home at 8 p.m. and she worked near full-time as well. Her commitment to me was insane.

Both my parents have sacrificed so much for me and my football. Mum put in some superhuman hours while I was a teenager playing in Brisbane. Dad also worked six days a week but when I got my L plates, he would make sure he finished work in time to sit with me in the car while I drove to training. When I was first starting to learn on a manual, we all went to an empty car park to practise. Dad sat in the front and Mum in the back, often with a glass of wine, and we'd all bunny-hop around together as I tried to figure out the clutch. We laughed non-stop. It's one my favourite memories. Mum and Dad created the best upbringing for both my brother and me. More recently, I have found myself trying to make a mental note of some of the things they did for us and our little family holiday traditions, so that they are at the ready when I have kids one day. I worry that, because we are not the most forward with our feelings, I'll never be able to properly thank them for everything they have done for me. I hope they know how grateful I am and will always be.

2.
School Days

I moved schools quite a bit. The simplest reason for that is I wasn't the best student. My brother stayed at Marymount College throughout his entire education whereas I only lasted there until Year 7. Marymount was a co-ed school and my tomboy beginnings continued into my social life in the playground. I hung out with boys and boys only, playing football and handball, and generally feeling superior to the groups of girls doing nothing except chatting in a circle. When I was 12, school sport was split by gender and that forced me to gel with some of the girls in my year group.

Still, I was getting into a little bit of trouble – enough for my parents to consider a change in school. I think they thought I was hanging out with the wrong people. The truth was more like me just being a little shit. I always wanted to be outside. I hated sitting in a classroom. I just wasn't that kind of kid. I was relatively bright and took a liking to maths, but it played second fiddle to sport and friends every time.

Mum put me into another private school, St Andrews College, where I joined in Year 8 and lasted until Year 11. That was the year I returned from a Young Matildas trip in Vietnam with a laser pointer. There were really fun markets selling lots of little gadgets, such as silly watches or fake Beats headphones, which was all very cool for a 16-year-old. A handful of us bought a laser pointer, and I just had to bring my cool new toy to school to show everyone. During a school assembly, I showed a friend, and he thought it might be a good idea to shine it on our principal's head while he was delivering his morning speech to the whole school. The principal did not appreciate it.

The last straw came when I plagiarised my science assignment – we were supposed to do it in pairs, and I took that a little too literally. As you might imagine, I got into deep shit for that. The school gave me the choice of redoing the assignment or 'looking at other schools'. I don't think they thought mum would choose the latter, but she did, and I deserved it. I would have done the same.

I don't know why I didn't apply myself to school as much as I should have. If I could go back now, I would take it a lot more seriously. I think I was so caught up in sport, and I wanted to be anywhere but the classroom. It's not like I was the devil – honestly, it was just a lack of concentration. I never missed a class or skipped school, but I just never took notes (somehow I still got As and Bs in maths).

When Mum pulled me out of that school, she sent me to Palm Beach Currumbin State High School (PBC). I only had to get through Year 12 to graduate – luckily for me, it was the best one yet, because they had a sports excellence programme. It was where surfers Mick Fanning and Joel Parkinson went to school, and Cody Walker and Kevin Proctor and a bunch of other NRL and AFL players. Jahrome Hughes was in my year group and was my soon-to-be best friend.

SHAQUILLE BOND, friend

We first met in health class. The teacher introduced Kenz to everybody, she sat next to me and we got talking. One of my first memories was how taken aback she was when my mobile phone rang during class. I just picked it up and answered it as if it was nothing. She had come from a strict private school and couldn't believe what she was seeing. The teacher asked me if everything was okay and said something along the lines of, 'It's all good, Sir. It's just my mum.' Then I finished the call and hung up. At lunchtime that day, I brought Kenz over to my friends and introduced her, and did that high school thing where you're like, 'She's in our group now.' Ever since then, we've been really close. We have similar personalities and both love sport, so we just hit it off. I was in PBC's sports excellence programme for basketball, so we were both active and just loved hanging out and going to the beach – all the normal stuff you do when you're a teenager. Kenz is just so easy to get along with. She's just so funny and charismatic. You can't be mad at her even if you want to be – she's just so likeable. We've always found it so hard to be serious when we're together because so much of our friendship is taking the piss out of ourselves and each other.

The main thing we don't have in common is rugby league teams. My pop was originally from Redfern, so even though our whole family lives up in Queensland now, we're all South Sydney supporters. So I hate the Brisbane Broncos. And State of Origin is always a lot of fun because she's die-hard Queensland and I'm die-hard NSW. Whenever she was back home around that time, she would come to watch it with my family. My aunty set up half the place with maroon streamers and the other half with blue streamers, and we'd eat footy food and get really mean with each other while the game was on – then love each other again afterwards. We did it with club footy, too. When former Rabbitohs captain Adam Reynolds moved to the Broncos, Kenz knew I was devastated, so she really played on that. Then it was my turn to give her grief after the Penrith Panthers came back to beat her beloved Broncos in the 2023 Grand Final, which is still a sore subject if we're being honest.

Because Kenz has spent so much of the past few years overseas, I've really only got to see her twice a year, when she comes home. But as soon as we're in the same room, it's as if no time has passed. It's one of those friendships that is so low maintenance and easy to slip back into.

Because I was born in February, my birthday was one of the first in my year group. That meant I got my licence first and was the one to drive us everywhere. My friends had designated seats in my car. Shaq always got the front and Liv and Jacinta sat in the back. One day, Jacinta really wanted to ride shotgun so we let her. That day, we went through the McDonald's drive-thru to get an ice-cream cone. As I was driving off, I went over a speed bump and Jacinta dropped the cone straight into the cup holder. The soft serve splattered everywhere – it took so long to clean. Jacinta was never allowed in the front again.

One person who had a big influence on me at PBC was Kate Gleeson, my coach and teacher in the football stream of the sports excellence programme. We first crossed paths at a schoolgirls' carnival. She was the coach to the older South Coast team; my friends in that team would always say how cool and how good a coach she was. She was one of the most selfless people I have ever met. I don't think I would have got through school without her. I was away a lot with the Young Matildas during my last terms of Year 12 – she did everything she could to keep me up to date with my subjects and make sure I didn't fall behind.

Kate could make people laugh whenever she walked into a room but at the same time had a knack for sensing when something was wrong with a student and took time to help whoever it was. Even after I graduated, she let me come back and train with the girls some mornings, because she knew how much I enjoyed it.

Kate died on 18 June 2014 from bowel cancer. She was diagnosed just as I was finishing Year 12 and passed a couple of years later when it got into her blood. It was a massive shock, because she was so fit and healthy. Kate was a huge advocate for women's football and had experienced the struggles firsthand in the QAS and with the many schoolgirls she taught. I just know she'd be going absolutely nuts with pride at how far the sport has come now. I wish she was here to see it.

3.

A Taste of the Big Time

I arrived at the QAS to an atmosphere I can only describe as intimidating. I was 16 when the tough nuts of the squad were in their 20s. I'm talking Kim Carroll, Karla Reuter and Clare Polkinghorne. God, I was petrified of Polks. They were the established girls and they weren't going to make it easy on the new kids coming in.

At the start of each training session, we usually did a rondo drill, which is a bit like that childhood game 'monkey in the middle'. A group of players form a circle around one or a couple of other players, who try to win the ball back as it is passed around them. If a player in the middle wins the ball, they typically swap places with the player who lost it. Coaches like this drill because it activates players both physically and mentally, and gets them thinking on their toes. We used one-touch passing, which meant if you stuffed up that touch you were probably going to end up in the middle. Well, Elise Kellond-Knight and Tameka Yallop used to smack the ball at me as hard as they could so I would have no chance of controlling the ball. They found it hilarious and the more they did it the funnier it became. They were totally just having a laugh and there was no harm intended; I was just young and surrounded by older, cooler people. And to be honest, I love that they did that. These days, everybody is so cautious with the younger generation. To be clear, I believe safeguarding is a must to protect players from genuine bullying and other forms of abuse. I guess what I am saying is that some things just aren't the same anymore. There was something about being a teenager and a little bit scared to come in for training, thinking, 'Shit, I better be on my game today, otherwise I'm getting it.'

When you earned their respect, it felt so good. I'll never forget when it happened with Polks. We were playing a friendly game. I was in goal and had come out for a cross, which was something I didn't usually do because I was still learning and not very good yet. But I ventured quite far out for this particular cross, took it with no problem and hit the deck. When I looked up, Polks was just staring at me. Then she said, 'Can you do that every time?' and helped me up off the ground. It was her way of saying, 'That was sick – keep doing that.' But it was the way she said it that made me want to improve so much quicker so I could keep impressing the older players.

The funny thing was that I was only just learning who these players were. I didn't know them as Matildas – I didn't really know of any Matildas. I just knew that Polks was my captain at the QAS. And while she might not have been the biggest voice in the changeroom, when she spoke, you listened. She later became my captain at Brisbane Roar and co-captain of the Matildas, and she was the person I looked to for inspiration and composure during high-pressure situations. I remember the way I viewed Polks as a skipper and hoped I could carry myself in a similar way.

Back then, I felt pretty misunderstood. I will admit that when I was younger, I could have sometimes been better in terms of my application. But I feel the way I acted was often misconstrued by coaches. I am a naturally happy person – I like to laugh and have a fun time with my friends. Over the years, there have been times, say, during a training session, when I have laughed or joked, and that has been perceived as a sign that I either am not taking football seriously or believe myself to be more talented than I actually am. This narrative gathered a lot of steam while I was young and before I had even considered I might be able to make a career out of playing football.

The first instance was a biggie and it almost cost me my entire future. It happened about a week after I had started training at the QAS. Some of the girls came up to me. I wasn't really a part of their crew because they were all based in Brisbane. But one blurted out, 'You're on the camp email.' I had no idea what they were talking about. For starters, I wasn't reading any emails because I didn't have an email address – Mum always put hers down whenever we had to fill out forms. I also didn't know what 'camp' was. The girl telling me about the 'camp email' seemed to know all about it, though. She said it was at the Australian

Institute of Sport (AIS) and went for four days. I know this is going to sound ridiculous but the only camps I knew about were the holiday camps I went to as a kid. The kind where you rock up, do a bit of training and get Subway for lunch. I confirmed with Mum that she had received the 'camp email' and so I got some things packed and prepared to go along. Those of us attending had to wear our Queensland tracksuits for the flight down to Canberra. I didn't love my Queensland tracksuit, so I thought I would make it look cooler by pulling the pants up to my knees. As I was getting ready to disembark the plane, a woman wearing a coach's uniform who I'd never seen before looked me up and down and said, 'Are you going to walk off the plane looking like that?'

I must have looked at her as if she was mad, because she told me in a very abrupt manner, 'Pull your pants down.' When we arrived at the AIS, we were staying in the dorms on site, so it still never clicked that this might be a Matildas development team (spoiler alert: it was). The Queensland girls were treating it very seriously but the Queensland girls treated everything very seriously. When I walked in, I saw the NSW girls laughing and having a good time. That didn't look very serious at all. Caitlin Foord, Alanna Kennedy, Emily van Egmond and Nicola Bolger looked pretty fun, I thought. I instantly knew I would get along with them. I ended up rooming with Nicola and, because she and Emily were good friends, struck up a good rapport with Emily, too. She was actually playing for the Matildas at this point and straddling both the senior and junior teams. In effect,

I had accidentally started hanging out with two of this squad's main starters. That is where it started. The coaches started asking: who did this upstart think she was socialising with these top dogs?

The whole camp was surreal – I just didn't understand what was happening. I had never been in an environment like this before – a week prior, I was still training in a park with Paul Jackson – and I didn't understand what was expected of me. I didn't know this would be the last camp from which to be selected for pre-qualifiers for the 2010 Under-17 Women's World Cup, which would have meant a trip to Thailand. The penny sort of dropped during a training session. The goalkeeper coach was a guy named Paul Jones. He was based in Canberra and was working with Lydia Williams, who was already with the Matildas as a back-up for Melissa Barbieri, so on this day she trained with the under-17s, from which the Junior Matildas would be selected. At one point, we were doing a drill where we took turns in goal. As Lydia's turn was due to end and mine to begin, she jogged out of the goal and I started to walk in. Jonesy, as we call him, looked at me and said, 'Forget it, next.' I asked if he wanted me to do the drill and he said, 'Are you really going to walk?'

PAUL JONES, coach

Macca's first national team camp was the start of what would become a strong friendship with the cool kids, Caitlin and Emily. Because Macca was hanging out with those two, who are outfield players and start training later than the goalkeepers, she turned up late to her first

45

national team goalkeeper session. I explained to her that this is not really acceptable but that I was happy to give her the benefit of the doubt on the basis she didn't understand that national team camp was pretty serious. Macca did well enough in training to show me she had some talent. It was raw but there was something there. The following day, Macca was late once more, to our second session. Once again, she had been hanging out with Emily and Caitlin. I had a strong word with her to explain this was poor. The day after that, she was late for session three for the same reason. At this time, I believed she needed an attitude realignment. So I took her out of the goalkeeper session and assigned her shuttle runs instead – two repeats of:

Touch line to six-yard box and back – 12 yards
Touch line to penalty spot and back – 24 yards
Touch line to 18-yard box and back – 36 yards
Touch line to centre-circle edge and back – 100 yards
Touch line to halfway line and back – 120 yards
Touch line to centre circle opposite side of halfway line
   and back – 140 yards
Touch line to opposite 18-yard box and back – 180 yards
Touch line to opposite penalty spot and back – 192 yards
Touch line to opposite six-yard box and back – 208 yards
Touch line to opposite touch line and back – 220 yards
Approximate total distance: 2464 yards (2.25 kilometres)

Macca was crying when she finished the run. It wasn't that far but her fitness wasn't great. I think it sunk in that she might have blown her chance with the national team. I had a strong phone conversation with her QAS coach, Jeff Hopkins, with Macca stand-ing beside me so she could hear. I told him she was never going to return if she continued to waste my time. Straight afterwards, I called Jeff privately, telling him if we could get her on the straight and narrow, she could be very special. Jeff called me a couple of months later to say her application and attitude had dramatically changed and ask if we would bring her back into camp. Staj [Alen Stajcic] and I discussed bringing her back in, which ended up being a pretty good decision. I could be wrong but I think I might have been the coach who had a significant impact on her future. After Macca came back into camp, she became special to me. I knew she had the potential; she just needed to understand that maturity takes guidance and time.

When I got back to the QAS, Jeff couldn't understand what had happened, because he had seen my application until that point. I tried to explain that I didn't fully understand what 'camp' meant. Jeff carries himself pretty quietly a lot of the time but he gave it to me a bit during this chat. He told me it wasn't good enough, that I needed to start tak-ing my football more seriously and that this sport could be my career if I wanted it to be. He told me that my selec-tion for that development camp was effectively my ticket to Thailand – but I had blown it. It was basically a stern talking-to to wake me up a bit. And it did. Casey Dumont was Brisbane Roar's starting goalkeeper at the time and I felt a bit of a fire to compete for her spot. Jeff really advocated for me after that, to help me get back into the national set-up.

JEFF HOPKINS, coach

As a young player, Mackenzie had a little bit of what you might call GCA: Gold Coast Attitude. She had a lot of talent and the attitude to back it up. You need that as a goalkeeper. It's an essential ingredient to be a top performer. Most top goalkeepers have a little bit of something different in them – a bit of something special. She definitely had that and I think at times it was misread by some people – when you get to know her, she's a good person and comes from a good family.

She's just got that little bit of cheek. Mackenzie would be one of the kids sitting at the back of the school bus, for sure. She wants to enjoy herself while she's working hard and she did always work hard while in my programme. Football can be quite lonely for a goalkeeper, even in a team environment, and everyone needs a kind word and a bit of reassurance now and then. Sometimes, if you believe in someone, you've got to stand up for them, and that's what I did.

She was definitely a super talent. A couple of things stood out when I first saw her play. The first was her size – she was a physical specimen. And the second, more importantly, was that she could play. She could join in with the outfield players and was very comfortable with the ball at her feet, which has become more and more important in modern goalkeeping. It's been so nice to sit back and watch her kick on to a completely new level.

About six months later, I was called up to the under-20s, called the Young Matildas, and had a lot more training under my belt. But my first and last chance with the Junior Matildas remains probably my biggest learning curve. The girls still talk about it to this day.

4.

Mates

Alanna Kennedy had an energy about her. During that development camp I was mainly socialising with Nicola and Emily but, because Alanna was friends with both of them, she was hanging around a bit, too. I thought she was cool and funny, and wanted to engineer an interaction between us that might lead to a friendship. The way I attempted to do this ended up being pretty awkward and funny in its own right. In the AIS dorms, there is a common room and one evening after dinner I walked past and could see her sitting in there on her own. I walked in, thinking we might naturally start chatting. As I did, I realised she was on the phone but, by the time I'd registered it was already too late to turn around without it being obvious I was only there to speak to her. So I kept walking and pretended I was doing my own thing and sat down. Except that I wasn't – and I didn't have anything to make me look busy. Still, I did my best until she finally hung up. We did start talking, and it turned out to be the start of a beautiful friendship – and the source of a long-running joke.

ALANNA KENNEDY

I was on the phone to a friend – it wasn't a serious chat. She sort of knew that it was okay for her to be in there. She's wasn't super weird, listening into a business call or anything. But she hovered around waiting for me to get off the phone. After I got off, we started chatting and bantering, and it was obvious we enjoyed each other's humour. We became literally best mates from the get-go. I'd already known Caitlin for years and we were really close; Mac jumped into that little crew with us, Sam and Emily and a few others. We were obviously all in the team together but we would also hang out away from camp whenever we could. We would occasionally visit her on the Gold Coast and other times she would come down to Sydney.

Caitlin lived up the road from my nana in Wollongong, where my mum is originally from. It's funny because, as Nana got older, Mum flew down quite a bit to visit and check on her. She always wanted me to come but, being a teenage kid, I found the concept of spending a full weekend at Nana's house a bit boring. That all changed as soon as I found out Caitlin was there – I wanted to go with Mum all the time then. That sounds terrible, because I loved my nana. It was more that I couldn't believe my luck that this cool new friend was suddenly so accessible, despite geography. While we were down there, I would go over to Caitlin's during the day and Mum would pick me up in time for dinner.

CAITLIN FOORD

Christmas in particular was always fun because Macca would be down at her nana's and I would be at home, so we would go to the beach, ride skateboards, go to the store. Once we were old enough, we'd go out on Christmas Eve and do what normal friends do outside of football.

Whenever we went around to see Macca's nan, we'd have to knock really hard because her hearing wasn't the best. We would be banging on the door and you would peek through the blinds and she'd be just sitting there watching the TV. Then she would finally come and would make us tea as nanas do. She had all the biscuits, all the lollies – she would grab everything out. 'You want some of this? You want some of this?' And Mac would be like, 'No, thanks, Nan. It's okay.' But obviously she couldn't hear, so more would keep coming out and we were just trying not to laugh. She was very, very cute and always welcoming. She'd be so happy to see Macca as well because it wasn't often that she was around.

We were quite young then, probably 16. During one trip to Wollongong, Lans, Nicola and Teigen Allen all came down to see Cait and me, and we all went to Jamberoo Action Park. It was called Jamberoo Recreation Park back then and I still remember the daggy South Coast ads that ran the slogan 'where you control the action'. We rode the go-karts and went on the chairlift. The ridiculous things we got up to as a group. When we see old photos of us together, we realise how lucky we are to have met so young through football. In reality, we were also best friends outside of football. It certainly made the various Young Matildas and Matildas camps that followed a lot of fun.

ALANNA KENNEDY

I love the three of us to bits. We can just do the dumbest things together and make it fun. We'd even just sit in each other's rooms, sometimes not even talking. Whenever there's time to kill or something, we're always together. If Mac was going to dinner, she'd walk past my room and knock on my door, and we'd go together. On the bus heading to training, if I'm not sitting next to Mac, I'm sitting next to Cait. And if they're sitting together, I'm annoyed that they're together and I'm not there, too.

While I was in the under-20s, we never qualified for any major tournaments but I enjoyed that time because I actually got to play and go on some fun trips to places such as China, Japan, Vietnam, Myanmar – most of Asia, really. Plus, all my friends were in the under-20s. Of course, that meant I got into trouble on the regular, breaking curfew and staying in others' rooms when I shouldn't have been. I was pretty immature.

I made my senior debut in late 2012. The coach at the time, Tom Sermanni, had already called me up that year as a back-up for a tour of the United States. In November, I was selected again for the Women's East Asian Cup in China. This time, Lydia was injured and Bubs (Melissa Barbieri) was pregnant. It was still a surprise when, during our team meeting on the eve of our preliminary-round match against Taiwan, Tom put up the starting line-up and I was in it.

I was like, 'Wait, what?' but no one else batted an eyelid. Tom is very chilled out. A Glaswegian former midfielder then in his late-50s, he had overseen the Matildas for about a decade and given a lot of my contemporaries – and the generation before us – their debuts. It meant he was a bit of a father figure to many of the girls. I didn't have time to develop that kind of relationship with him, because I only came into the set-up in time for his last few games in charge, but I really appreciated how calm he made my experience. He told me I would make my international debut and to enjoy it. That was that. Of course, I was nervous but I was also excited. Also in the starting line-up was Sam, Cait, Steph Catley and Emily, and Kyah Simon and Kate Gill. Lans, Polks and Katrina Gorry were among those on bench, so everything at least felt familiar.

Often the best thing to settle my nerves is an early touch or save. It came during the first half at Shenzhen Stadium when a cross came in and I ran out to catch it. It was a decent grab and the girls gassed me up and got around me for it. After that, the ball was pretty much down the other end for most of the match. We won 7–0. In many ways, it was the perfect debut. A low-stakes match in an inconsequential tournament that wasn't televised in Australia. There were no eyes on the game, which meant there was no one to judge me. I had, by then, started to understand that playing for the Matildas was a big deal, realising just how far it's come and the position we find ourselves in now. These days, players are debuting in front of 50,000 at a stadium and more watching live on television. Some new players thrive in that situation. Take Clare Hunt, whose debut in the 2023 Cup of Nations was so sure-footed she has started in central defence for almost every match since. For me, still 18 and less psychologically equipped, I appreciated that Tom was able to make such a big moment feel low key. It was only afterwards that I properly realised what it meant: I was going to play for the Matildas now.

It also clicked that the kids my age who were getting into the team were also playing in what was then known as the W-League. I had just finished my first season with Perth Glory and decided I would give it my best shot in Australia's top-flight domestic league.

5.
Glory and United

Schoolies was coming up and we had booked a 10-day trip to Bali. I had only been at PBC for one year, so I was a late addition to the friendship circle. But they asked me if I wanted to come and I jumped at it. We booked our flights and accommodation, and we were maybe a week or two away from leaving when Jeff approached me one day at the QAS. He'd had a call from Perth Glory's W-League coach, Jamie Harnwell. They needed a goalkeeper for the upcoming season – would I be interested? There wasn't even a discussion to be had. I knew immediately I would be going to Perth and not to Bali, and I was on the plane less than a fortnight after finishing Year 12. I was playing a couple of weeks after that.

JAMIE HARNWELL, coach

It was my first season of coaching. I'd come into it fairly late in the piece, after playing for Glory myself. We didn't have a goalkeeper as such, or one who we would call a first choice, and so Jeff offered me

Macca to come over and play for Perth for the season. It was her first real chance – her first time being away from home and first time playing at that level. I don't believe Macca came to Perth initially to train because she was still finishing school at the time. She and another player from the QAS, defender Erika Elze, flew direct to Melbourne and met with the team the day before our round-one game against Melbourne Victory. We had a bit of a kick about in the local park and then she was thrown straight into the deep end. She made her debut without necessarily knowing any of the other players around her.

Macca was so young but she did have a confidence about her, and her height gave her a presence as soon as she walked into the room. She made mistakes in our first season but we weren't a particularly good team either. We won two games and lost eight, and finished second to last. So she was under a lot of pressure most games, because we were struggling with our backs to the wall and trying to improve on what we were. It would have been pretty tough to move across the country at that age, be put into a house with three or four other players and have to look after herself across a three- or four-month period.

I was definitely out of my comfort zone. I had watched the W-League the year before at Brisbane Roar and never expected myself to be playing in it the following year. Before that first game, I talked to Brianna Davey – at the time, she played for our opponent Melbourne Victory and I was very nervous about my first game. She told me I'd be fine and not to worry. She kept saying, 'No pressure. There's no pressure.' In the end, I played quite well – after the game, she came up to me and said, 'See, it's not that bad.'

I loved it from that point on. I was ready to play every game. I wasn't nervous, which helped. It was exciting.

I knew Marianna Tabain and some of the other under-20s girls, and I was in a house with three other girls who were quite a bit older. I mean, they were in their 20s, but still had a good few years on me – New Zealand international Emma Kete, Norwegian Lisa-Marie Woods and English defender Katie Holtham. At night, they would give me the strangest expressions as I sat down to eat. 'You're not having that for dinner . . .' they would say, looking at my butter and Vegemite on toast with disdain. I couldn't cook, so I ate toast every night. Mum used to ring me up and relay easy recipes over the phone to try to teach me how to make something with more nutrition but I was honestly quite happy with the toast – I really like toast and it was easy. The girls weren't having it, though, so they cooked for me sometimes and made me clean up in return. Then, as I made more friends within the team, I had dinner at other people's places, too.

I liked the social aspect of it and living away from home. But my money ran out very, very quickly. This was my first contract – I was paid $1000 for about four months. The club paid for my rent and a car that all the girls in our house shared (given my age, I practically never saw it). At 17, I was pretty stoked to have a grand in my bank account but it was gone within two or three weeks. I went shopping one time and it was practically gone. Mum gave me a spray about that but then she and Dad helped me make ends meet while I was there. They wired me petrol money to contribute to carpooling and enough to cover my food each week. Other than that, though, I loved it. Until round seven, when we were hammered 11–0 by Alen Stajcic's Sydney FC at Leichhardt Oval.

JAMIE HARNWELL

It was a horrible feeling for everybody. I'd never been involved in something like that as a player or as a new coach, and to walk off the field after that game was pretty demoralising. We finally had our strongest team together – all our internationals were fit and playing – and we were 2–0 down at half-time. I still remember my half-time team talk. It was one of encouragement, telling the players that we could get back in this. Well, by the 60th minute mark, it was 7–0 and I had made all my substitutions. There was literally nothing I could do aside from sit there and watch and hope that the final whistle would be blown sooner rather than later.

ALEN STAJCIC, Sydney FC coach

Mac was bawling her eyes out. I remember picking her up off the ground that day. Renee Rollason scored a hat-trick. Kylie Ledbrook scored a hat-trick. Leena Khamis scored a hat-trick. In the second half, it was goal after goal – practically every attack was a goal. Then, in the 80th minute, I put Kyah Simon on. She had been 2010–11 player of the year and golden boot but was just coming back from an injury, so I gave her 10 minutes at the end. I remember Jamie Harnwell looking towards the halfway line, seeing her, and just putting his head in his hands. I could imagine him thinking, 'We're 9–0 down, it's the 80th minute and the best player in the league is coming on. We're fucked.' I had a little chuckle to myself.

My parents had driven down to Sydney for it. I was so embarrassed because Sydney FC was full of my mates. I was crying after the game. Mum and Dad were really supportive and probably just upset that I was upset – I don't think they were too fazed about the result. I told them I didn't want to be there anymore. I don't really get homesick – I am usually settled no matter where I am – but I was feeling pretty overwhelmed right then.

STEVE ARNOLD

During the game, I was in line waiting to buy a drink and kept hearing loud cheers, because the ball obviously kept going in the net and the Sydney crowd were loving it. Afterwards, she was pretty upset, saying, 'The whole thing's crap. I'm not getting back on that bus and going back to Perth.' As she was saying this, the coach is standing right behind us. That stopped her talking and Jamie managed to get her back on the bus. He was really good and believed in her a lot.

JAMIE HARNWELL

It was a character-building moment. You've got two directions to go in after something like that: you either curl up and go, 'Look, this isn't for me,' or you continue fighting and trying to improve. She did the latter – thankfully. We did that as a club a little bit more as well. But it certainly caused some challenges within the playing group. A couple of our internationals who were living with Macca had an argument during training that eventually got into a physical altercation at the house. Macca stepped in between them and broke it up. Both those players moved on from the club after that but it would have been a tough thing for a 17-year-old to have to deal with.

The fight happened one day after a training session, during which they'd had a disagreement. The argument carried on back at the house. It was pretty hectic at the time because I was still so young and I had to get in the middle of them to get one away from the other.

STEVE ARNOLD

The club made sure they got in contact with us before Mackenzie did, because I think they were dead scared we might be so shocked that we'd get her on a plane and bring her home. We did go to visit her after that, just to check she was okay and see what the hell was going on over there. The house was pretty basic. The place was in darkness just about and there was hardly any furniture – maybe a couple of beanbags and a TV in the living room. The whole set-up was pretty sparse. No one mowed the lawn so the grass was up past your ankles. And when we walked into Mackenzie's room, I'd never seen so many empty water bottles in my life. The whole floor was covered in empty water bottles she had dropped and left there.

A move to Canberra the next season felt like the most natural thing to do. United were 2011–12 premiers and champions and, after my humbling experience in Perth, I didn't mind the idea of being part of a winning team.

We had a pretty good squad, with names including reigning golden boot Michelle Heyman, Hayley Raso, Ellie Brush and Caitlin Cooper. And Lyds had done her ACL while playing in Sweden, which meant I would probably be the starting keeper. Trudy Burke had signed as the other goalkeeper and we both trained with Jonesy, who we had far more to do with than our head coach, Jitka Klimková. Trudy and I became good friends and spent every spare second together. When it came to the actual football, I really just went through the motions. I'd like to say there was a lofty reason for this – some innate sense or profound truth I was yet to learn – but in all probability it was just a mix of my personality and lack of maturity. In everything I did, I went with the flow. Perth Glory want to sign me? Okay, let's go to Perth. Canberra United? Sure, why not? I played almost every game for Canberra in 2012–13 and won my first goalkeeper of the year award.

PAUL JONES

We trained together four to five times a week – two sessions with the team and another two to three one-on-one sessions – working on her technical skills and her understanding of the game. We also played squash a couple of times a month as a form of cross training. These sessions were designed to help Macca with her reaction times, short-distance movement and decision-making.

After the season, Jonesy said it would be in my best interest to stay in Canberra and continue training with him and some of the kids from his academy. He told Trudy the same thing. It did make sense. I didn't know if Brisbane Roar had a goalkeeper coaching set-up and, even if they did, how I would fit into it? I was still a nobody. And, after all, Jonesy was the Matildas' goalkeeper coach – training with him could give me more exposure to get into the team. In the short term, at least, that didn't work. The manager at the time, Hesterine de Reus, did not seem to warm to me and I didn't play again for the Matildas until 2015, which was well after Staj had taken over. At the time, though, it was the obvious next step and my parents thought so too.

The only hitch was that they were still not keen on the whole football-as-a-career concept. A big part of that was the lack of opportunities in the women's game. There was hardly a visible career path and many players had other jobs out of financial necessity. My break at the QAS certainly gave them cause for hope but Mum was still a big advocate for me to go to university and get a proper job. She was a realist – the counterpoint to my nonchalance – and she was kind of right. They wanted me to have something to fall back on if football didn't work out. My resumé was empty. I had never had a job. Before I left home, I applied for a few just to make Mum happy, handing my practically blank CV out to a sandwich shop and a coffee shop. But I couldn't do any weekend or evening shifts because of football. The whole thing was more an exercise in placation.

More immediately, Mum and Dad didn't want to pay for my rent and pay for coaching in Canberra if I had not committed to at least one constructive pursuit on the side. Uni was never up my street. I couldn't figure out what I wanted to do. I know that sounds like a cop-out, but if it didn't involve football and friends (and football friends!), I was a bit directionless. In the end, I opted to do my Cert 4 in Fitness at TAFE. I moved in with Canberra's team manager, Maria, and her two little girls, and began my off-season. I trained three or four nights a week with Jonesy and went to TAFE some mornings. And when I say some, I mean I barely showed up. I also ended up playing for an NPL team whenever they needed an extra player, just to keep fit and earn a tiny bit of money. Not that any-body knew – I had to keep it quiet because I was playing in the outfield and I definitely was not allowed to be doing that. I was up front and I was good at it. It was honestly so much fun. It felt so different to playing goalkeeper because there was no pressure – no one expects anything of you.

(I experienced this one more time, in 2021, when I played 20 minutes in midfield for West Ham. It was a fourth-round FA Cup game against lower-league side Chichester & Selsey. I was only just coming back from an MCL injury and hadn't even been back on the pitch as a goalkeeper. But our squad was lean from injuries and tired bodies from the previous weekend's match. We were also trying to keep players fresh for an important game com-ing up, so I offered my services if needed. I was subbed on in the 68th minute and had a ball. I was definitely off the pace but didn't feel out of place with the ball at my feet. We won 11–0 and Emily – who was with us at the time – scored four goals. There was a bit of chat in other camps and in the media about disrespecting our opponents but we were genuinely low on numbers and had to make do with what we had.)

Other than that, there wasn't much else to do. We went to the shops sometimes, or the movies. Trudy wanted to learn to skateboard and I already did a bit, just at the park and on the street, so we went to the skate park every now and then. I remember we were trying to learn to drop in and we picked it up relatively quickly. Trudy must have been feeling particularly confident with it, because I turned up to training with Jonesy one day and she wasn't there. It turned out she had gone to the skate park on her own the night before, fallen backwards and broken her wrist. Jonesy was fuming and neither of us went to the skate park again.

Jonesy was probably the most influential coach of my career, because he was a constant from when I was 16 until I was 25. I owe a lot to him. He knew what he was doing, but he did have this old-school attitude of wanting to teach you a lesson if he didn't approve of something. But then he'd pull you aside and tell you why he did what he did, and how it was going to make you a better player. Then I'd think, 'That kind of makes sense. I just need a better attitude.' The other players watching would later tell me the way he treated us keepers was not okay. But because Jonesy had explained his reasons, I would say he was just trying to get the best out of us. The cycle sort of went like that.

He was a very good coach. I'll put my hand up and say he taught me a lot, and I think a big part of who I am as a goalkeeper comes down to what he did for my development. He always got the best out of me. I'm just not sure if his approach was the best for some goalkeepers. But in saying that, if you saw how I was as a kid, maybe I did need that kind of management. Whatever the answer, I have such a hard skin because I dealt with that. I'm also a perfectionist when it comes to getting things right.

6.

Twist of Fate

My time in Canberra ended when Lydia completed her ACL rehab and returned to her rightful place as United's first-choice keeper, and when Western Sydney offered me a contract for the 2013–14 season. So, off I went to another new team in another new city. On paper, this Wanderers side was stacked. Heather Garriock was captain. Emily van Egmond. Alanna Kennedy. Kyah Simon. Catherine Cannuli. For an expansion club in its second season, it felt like a potentially title-winning side. The fact Lans was there meant guaranteed fun and the pay packet was a significant step up. My contract at Canberra United was about $3000, which was better than at Perth. But the Wanderers salary was going on $8000 – I thought that was everything. But my season was about to be derailed before it had even begun.

In mid-October, a few weeks before the W-League season was due to kick off, I went to Nanjing, China, with the Young Matildas. We were contesting the AFC U-19

Championship, which doubled as the final qualifiers for the 2014 Under-20 Women's World Cup. We had just lost our third successive game – 2–1 to host nation China – which ruled us out of World Cup calculations, though we still had another two to play to see out the tournament. The accident occurred as my teammate Amy Harrison and I were jogging from a recovery session back to the team bus, via a car park. At one point, I weaved between two cars to get from the road to the footpath and stepped up onto the path right where one car's metal number plate was jutting out at a sharp angle. As I made my diagonal half-leap onto the pavement and put my full weight through my right foot, the edge of the number plate ripped up through the outside of my right shin.

It felt like a scratch; there was next to no pain. But as I continued to run, I could feel something flapping. When I looked down, my leg was like an open piece of steak. You couldn't see the bone but you could see the flesh of my calf. There was blood everywhere. As soon as I clocked that, I fell to the ground and grabbed my leg to hold it close. I called out to Amy as she was about to get on the bus. She turned around, took one look at my leg and her face dropped. 'Get the physio,' I said. I was trying not to panic and avoiding looking down. Amy came back with the doctor, just as Jonesy caught up from behind.

PAUL JONES

When I arrived, she was on the ground with a towel over her leg holding the muscle together. I said I was sure it wasn't that bad.

She asked me to have a look and as she took the towel away from her leg, the muscle opened up. My reaction was, 'Holy fuck.' Macca saw my face and burst into tears.

The doctor taped up my calf and said we had to get to a hospital. The closest one we could find wasn't great. Everybody was freaking out. Nobody there spoke English. Nobody from our camp spoke Mandarin. I was taken into a room and ordered to get up onto a table that was still spattered with blots of blood from the last patient. I saw it at the same time as our doctor did and she said I was not to get onto that table under any circumstances. A lot of yelling ensued and Jonesy put his headphones over my ears and gave me his iPad to watch something, so I couldn't take any of it in. In the end, Football Federation Australia (FFA – as it was known then) got in touch with the Asian Football Confederation and sent me to another hospital about 90 minutes' drive away, where the AFC's head doctor was stationed. Once there, I had to go under general anaesthetic and had 15 internal stitches and 10 external stitches. I also had a tetanus shot and an X-ray to make sure no shards of number plate or paint were still inside my leg. After all of this, the doctor went back to the car park to take a photo of the offending number plate – some of my flesh was still hanging off it. I also still have evidence in the form of a proper pirate scar, complete with little dots on either side where the stitches were.

We had to stay five more days in China while the team played those last two fixtures, then I flew back to Sydney just in time for the Wanderers to effectively rule me out for three-quarters of the season. I returned a lot sooner than expected but just wasn't the same goalkeeper anymore. I'd lost my mojo. A combination of a new environment and new team, and a feeling of being rushed back cold with next to no training. There was also added pressure because Western Sydney had signed an emergency goalkeeper to replace me. She ended up being the starting keeper and the original back-up remained the back-up. It meant they didn't really need me back urgently and, when I had a shocker in my first game back, I was pretty much benched for the rest of the season.

At least my living arrangements were comfortable. For the whole season, I lived with Chloe Logarzo and her family in West Pennant Hills. She had been with me in the Young Matildas and we grew close. Amy Harrison and Olivia Price, who were at Sydney FC with Chloe, were good friends as well. Cait and Sam were playing for the Sky Blues too, and Lans was at the Wanderers with me. We all went out together a fair bit, sometimes to a club or a music festival if the timing was right between games. At the time, we thought we were so professional, on these lucrative contracts. In reality, we weren't earning much; we just had nothing to compare it to. The same went for some of the facilities, which could sometimes be a bit shitty. This didn't happen at the Wanderers but there were some instances during my time in the W-League when teammates had to get ready across the road from the match venue at a different facility because there wasn't any access to change-rooms at the stadium.

After my Wanderers contract finished, I almost had to beg Jamie to take me back at Perth. I had spent a season on my arse, which made me a less-than-attractive prospect for potential suitors. My Wanderers contract was only one season – they all were for a long time – so I technically no longer had a team. I also didn't have an agent, because none of us really did, and I think either Jonesy or Jeff must have got back in touch with Jamie and asked on my behalf. Thankfully, Glory needed a goalkeeper and he went out on a limb and signed me. Mum and Dad weren't keen for me to repeat my previous Perth living arrangements so Sam's parents, Roger and Roxanne, offered to have me for the season. Sam had returned home, where she would play for the next five years between stints in America's National Women's Soccer League (NWSL), and Cait had signed as well. The only missing link fell into place when Lans made a snap decision to join us. Before we knew it, we were all living with the Kerrs.

> **STEVE ARNOLD**
>
> They have been really good to us, the Kerrs. They have four children so they're used to plenty of kids around the house. Perth made the final that year so we went over for that. Roger showed us a good time – we went to all sorts of places and barely made the flight home the next day.

That season turned out to be my best yet – I won my second W-League goalkeeper of the year award. I put it down to the fact I was so happy off the field. On our days off, we walked the dogs on the beach, drank coffee and ate burgers at our favourite place, Missy Moos. Cait flew her dog Peach over to Perth for the season. Sam's dog had recently died but she got a new puppy in time for our arrival, so the dogs came everywhere with us. I love dogs but Alanna is not really a dog person. Hilariously, she would always pretend she liked them, even though she hated them in her room. Lans and I had our own rooms but hung out 24/7. Every night, we watched *Big Brother* together, which meant just about every night we also demolished an entire packet of Shortbread Creams. Every time we did that, we felt terrible and guilty, and promised ourselves never again. By the next night, we were back in the kitchen and opening the pantry to a magically replenished supply of Shortbread Creams. 'Oh God, the biscuits are back,' we'd groan, and then polish off the lot. There were a couple of actual meals we got pretty excited for, too. Chicken schnitzel and potato bake night was the stuff of legend, and we still talk about curry night. Rox made this butter chicken from a recipe that came from Roger's Indian mum.

ALANNA KENNEDY

Mac and I both loved reality shows – when we were younger, we'd just eat whatever the fuck we wanted, watch trash TV and go to training the next day. We would never do that now. I mean, don't get me wrong, I could still smash a packet of Shortbread Creams if I really wanted to. But it was just this weird life we led. Other kids our age were going to uni or starting jobs, and we were literally just going to training and then going to the beach. We got to hang out with each other all day. We were just so lucky.

When we weren't eating at home, we were going out to house parties and festivals. We probably shouldn't have been out every other weekend but we were winning and playing well so reasoned it made sense to keep doing it. We finished the season as premiers with 10 wins and two losses, and lost the grand final 3–1 to Canberra United. I stayed with Glory the following season, though it didn't reach the same heights in terms of form and fun. We finished second to last, with only three wins.

CAITLIN FOORD

Mac and I got really close during that second year, when Lans went back to Sydney and it was just the three of us. We had always got along well, but it clicked on another level when I was going through a difficult time and Mac helped me through it. It made our bond a lot stronger and that has remained to this day. We were also both young-ish and living away from home and it got to a point where we weren't necessarily really happy over there, but we had to be there. Two weeks before the end of the 2015–16 season, I broke my collarbone and said to Mac, 'I'm really sorry but this injury is a blessing in disguise for me. I'm going home and getting out of this.' Mac had a little quad tear at the time. It wasn't too bad but she wanted to make it worse so she could leave as well, so went and ran stairs to try to exacerbate it. It was like she couldn't do it without me. To be honest, if the roles were reversed, I probably would have done the same.

7.
The Next Level

As much as I believed that my play-in-the-day/party-at-night mindset did not affect my football, I think Staj had other ideas when he became Matildas coach in April 2014. He was initially drafted in as interim at the 11th hour, following the sacking of Hesterine de Reus, who had become the subject of a player revolt I was too young to fully understand. The situation left FFA with little choice other than to make a change less than a month out from the 2014 Asian Cup. Staj had won two W-League titles with Sydney; he was a hard coach but also one who cared a lot. I had assumed I'd be selected in his Asian Cup squad as one of the back-up goalkeepers. I assumed wrong. Staj could see right through me. He knew I thought I was a shoo-in and he wasn't going to just let me coast. On selection day, I had a text from Amy to say she had been cut. I hadn't heard a peep and started to wonder if I might have made it. It didn't take long for that bubble to burst. About a minute later, my phone rang and Staj's name popped up. He told me I too had been cut. I don't even remember the reason he gave because I sort of went into my head on first hearing the news. I am pretty sure he left me out to teach me a lesson and force me to pull my finger out, and a couple of conversations we have had since all but confirmed this. It wouldn't have made a difference to the team because, realistically, I would have only been the third goalkeeper anyway – I was never going to play. It just sucked because I still had to train with the team on the Gold Coast, in the knowledge they were all about to go on a cool trip to Vietnam.

PAUL JONES

Mackenzie has had her fair share of tough love from Staj and myself over the years. We knew she had the ability to play at a top level – the ability to be one of the best in the world. But she needed to get her attitude right. Sometimes, when Mackenzie was comfortable in the Matildas, she would go back to her old habits, not being as focused as she could be, not always working as hard as she should. But Staj knew that if she was left out of a squad for a training camp, she would come back more focused, more determined to get back in favour of the coaches.

The desired effect was achieved – I experienced a sudden shot of perspective. Playing – and even being selected – for the Matildas wasn't going to be a given if I continued treading water. And, judging by Mum's reaction, no Matildas meant more ultimatums about giving up on football and studying instead. In a way, I think she was testing me, too. I don't believe she would have followed through and actually made me stop playing but the seed of doubt was strong enough to prompt action. When I was growing up, I just made teams without much effort. I never really had to sacrifice anything. It sounds cocky but it became a drawback once there was genuine competition. My first rival was probably Casey Dumont, as we were both after the no. 3 position.

Casey also went to PBC but she was a couple of years ahead of me and graduated before I arrived. She was a quality W-League goalkeeper – one of my friends at the time asked if I looked up to her. My reflex reaction was to say that I didn't. Then I thought that maybe I should, so I went to a Brisbane Roar game and got her signature and put it up on my bedroom wall for a while. I took it down soon after that, when I felt like a fake, pretending to idolise somebody I didn't actually look up to. The only person in my life who fitted that category was Lockyer, so he got to stay. Then I started training with Casey at the QAS and I knew I was better than her. I wanted to do what she was doing. I liked her a lot as a person but didn't want to be her.

By the beginning of 2015, Bubs still hadn't played for Australia since having her daughter, which made Lydia and Bre the clear top-two keepers. Casey had been around the Matildas for a few years and was in the squad when they won the 2010 Asian Cup. She was also selected ahead of me for the 2014 tournament. I wanted to get back into reckoning in time for the 2015 World Cup.

My award-winning return season with Perth Glory in 2014 helped my case. I got some good news on 24 February 2015 – the day before my 21st birthday. I was out for lunch with Mum when Staj called. I knew the Cyprus Cup – an invitational tournament featuring mostly European teams and a few others, including Australia, South Korea, Canada, Mexico and South Africa – was approaching and I wasn't feeling optimistic. I had been in a recent Matildas training camp when I strained my quad. I have never had very good quads – a past scan had shown a lot of scar tissue and I tend to strain them more easily than most people. I tried to play through it, rubbing and banging my leg in the hope that would fix it. Our physio, Kate Beerworth, pulled me out just behind the goal and did some on-field tests. I didn't pass. It wasn't torn but my strength was limited. She eventually pulled me out of training, telling me there was no point in making it worse. I was upset and frustrated, believing this would probably rule me out of the Cyprus Cup – she tried to assure me it wasn't really an injury, just a precaution.

Days later, when Staj called, I had just been telling Mum how up in the air everything felt. I picked up the phone. 'How's your quad feeling?' he asked, before asking me if I would like to join the Matildas for the Cyprus Cup. He said a scan had shown my injury to be very minor. I couldn't believe it. I was leaving the next day – *on* my 21st birthday. Mum said we should have people over, so I invited my friends Shaq and Liv, and my nana and pop and aunty and uncle, and we all had takeaway pizzas and a birthday cake out the back. And then I flew to Cyprus.

Boy, was I in for a learning curve. Bre was the starting keeper at the time and she played our opening 1–0 win over the Netherlands. She also started our second game, against England. It was a freezing cold night at the GSP Stadium and, given there was no chance I would be playing, I was rugged up in my trackies and three jumpers and covered in blankets. I had settled in for the night, content to watch the game from the bench. Then, just after the hour mark, when we were 2–0 down, Bre got injured. Staj whirled around in his technical area and called for me to warm up. Panic set in immediately. I threw off the blankets in one fell swoop and started to get ready as fast as I could. I tried to take my tracksuit off over my boots but they wouldn't fit through. The more I tried, the more frantic everything felt. Once I was in just my shorts, I made a move to begin a warm-up run but Jonesy called me over. 'We don't have time,' he said. The physios were looking at Bre and we only had a couple of minutes tops before I was due in goal. Jonesy started kicking the ball to me to help me warm up quickly but, for some inexplicable reason, he picked a spot right in front of the England bench to do it. All the substitutes were staring as I tried to catch balls. I don't know if it was because I was facing them and could see their eyes on me, or that I was already so frazzled, but I shit you not, I could not catch a ball to save my life. I probably faced six volleys and caught one. With each one that slipped through my gloves, my embarrassment bubbled. I was trying so hard to appear chilled about the whole process when, beneath the surface, the opposite was true.

PAUL JONES

Macca dropped a simple catch and one of the England coaches made a comment along the lines of, 'Oops. Butterfinger goalkeeper.' For a person who is ready to play, it would be nothing. For a young goalkeeper coming on as a sub for the first time at international level, it was unnerving. It wasn't a very nice thing to say but that's international sport – you need to block out these types of comments.

I rushed to the halfway line, where I needed to be to enter the field of play, and stood next to Staj. He could obviously see how worked up I was, issuing a, 'Calm down, you'll be fine.' Then his gaze shifted down to my lower legs. 'Do you have your shin pads on?' Fuck. For the rest of my living days on this earth, I will not truly understand why I did what I did next. The only thing I can think of is I was so high on humiliation following my comedy of errors that perhaps I believed if I ignored this latest blunder it might just go away. I turned to Staj, put my finger to my lips and said, 'Shhh.' Staj, obviously, was having none of my 'I won't tell if you don't' bollocks and simply said, 'No, you need to go and get your shin pads.' My mortification peaked. I had to slink back over to our bench and wait for one of the girls to throw me the missing pieces of my kit. When I finally went on, still in my senseless state, I directly disobeyed orders. The doctor and coaching staff had decided my quad wasn't ready for a big goal kick and directed me to play out from the back instead. But I was suddenly determined to smack the ball long. My quad actually felt fine after doing it; my bosses on the bench were fuming. They couldn't figure out why I just wasn't listening. Computer said no once more in the 83rd minute, when a through ball hurtled towards me. I ran out to clear it at the same time as Jodie Taylor, who already had a brace, tried to run onto it. I beat her by a small margin, went to take the kick, and took a big air swing instead. The ball bounced clear over my leg and Taylor continued her run and passed it into the net to complete her hat-trick and England's 3–0 win.

The next day, in our review, Jonesy had a talk with me about always being ready to play, even when I'm not supposed to be playing. I feel sure he had delivered this same message before under less dramatic circumstances. It's amazing how a scarred ego can make stuff stick. That night has never left me. In every single match since, I have been as good as ready to run on at any moment. Even when it's cold, I do not wear long pants over my shorts. I usually have my shin pads on ready to go. It was one of the biggest learning curves of my career.

As it turned out, I started our final group game against Finland and then our fifth-place match against the Czech Republic, both comfortable victories that, of course, both felt significantly better. Then we spent a month in Italy preparing for the World Cup, which was due to start in Canada that June.

My inglorious England episode aside, I must have done something right, because I made the World Cup squad.

And, in a shock to everyone, Bri Davey did not. The selection meetings happened in May at Sydney's Valentine Sports Park, which is the home of Football NSW and where we trained and stayed before the tournament. I was stoked to be told I had made it at all. In my mind, I was in a fight for the third spot with Bubs, and Bri and Lyds had theirs locked up. When I bounced down to Bri's room to tell her the good news – that we would be going to the World Cup together – Steph and a couple of the other girls were already in there, perched on the bunk beds around a crying Bri. Steph looked up, saw me standing in the doorway, and asked if I could please give them a second. I left, a bit shocked at what had clearly just transpired. Bri was a friend and I felt terrible for her. Then I wondered: does this mean I could be second choice? This would be Bubs's fourth World Cup and she was at the time 35. A couple of weeks prior, I was hoping to be third choice; now I was seemingly in the discussion to start at a World Cup – and our opening match was against the USA. Before we left for the airport I made sure I saw Bri and gave her an extra hug. I knew exactly what she would be feeling.

Playing the States was always epic. For starters, they were the OG women's football powerhouse – champions of the inaugural Women's World Cup in 1991 and again in 1999, when 90,000 crammed into the Rose Bowl to watch the penalty-shootout final against China and to witness Brandi Chastain score the winning spot kick and complete her iconic shirt-off celebration. The USA had never once finished lower than third at a World Cup and were the undisputed women's football dynasty – they had slipped to world no. 2 for the previous six months but before that had been world no. 1 for six and a half years straight. They were the team to beat and had all the big stars: Megan Rapinoe, Abby Wambach, Carli Lloyd, Alex Morgan. Hope Solo was the goalkeeper and she had a good game. A few of our girls, such as Steph and Sam, had played club football with them in the US but I knew none of the team personally.

Realistically, I knew that Lydia would be the first choice to start this game. Until, that is, she sustained a minor injury. It wasn't a big deal, just one of those niggly things. But it was enough to rule her out of the game. All of a sudden, I was in the conversation. Not that anybody told me that at the time. But there can be little signs, like where you are positioned in training and whether you play in warm-up friendlies. For instance, I was in goal for a friendly against a boys' team just before the tournament, which I knew meant I was getting close. And guess what happened during this scratch match: one of the boys smacked me in the foot as I came out to clear a ball. I could hardly walk on it and had to leave the field immediately. It was then that Jonesy confirmed what I had suspected, revealing he and Staj were strongly considering throwing me in against the US but that they just couldn't risk it now given two goalkeepers were now dealing with niggles. I wasn't even that disappointed. I was just stoked that I was being talked about as a possibility.

Bubs played in the 3–1 loss, with Lyds and me watching from the bench. My knock turned out to be just an impact injury and I bounced back within a couple of days. But so did Lyds and she was the keeper selected for our second group match against Nigeria – a 2–0 win thanks to Kyah's brace. She also started our third group game – a 1–1 draw with Sweden, which sealed second place in our group – along with our 1–0 round-of-16 win over Brazil and quarter-final loss to Japan. I was okay with all of it – my headspace was still that I knew my place was behind Lyds and she played unreal. The pressure I felt during this time came more from what was happening around the fringes, in the dressing rooms and at training.

Coaches were still giving me a pretty hard time about my attitude. I cannot count how many times I was told I was too laid back, didn't want it enough, laughed too much, talked too much, thought I was better than I was, acted as if I was a starter when I wasn't, hung around the 'big dogs', hung around the 'cool kids'. I wouldn't say I believed all of what I was hearing but it did affect me substantially, and the hangover from each Matildas camp was felt in my outside life. The comments felt relentless. My young psyche didn't know how to process them in a logical manner. What I was being told did not match with my perception of myself and that was confusing. I didn't know how to *be* within the team environment. I never knew where I stood or how I should act. I became so self-conscious that I didn't actually act like myself a lot of the time. I was trying so hard to be this professional footballer but seemed to fail on every count. I just couldn't figure out what the coaches wanted so I could give it to them.

Even in the changerooms before games, I love dancing around and being a bit silly. The other girls enjoy doing the same thing. Then we switch on in time for the warm-up and everything gets serious. I make a conscious effort to avoid thinking too much about the game too early, because that stresses me out and I overthink the game. The mucking around helps me mentally, yet I wasn't allowed to do it because it appeared as if I wasn't concentrating. This went back to that idea that Sam was allowed to muck around because she goes out and scores goals and performs. Basically, she's Sam Kerr. And she *is* Sam Kerr – she's incredible. But the message was that we had to earn our own personalities through what we did on the field. Given I was never on the field, this was a perplexing concept. It was rough and it has haunted most of my Matildas career. The ironic result was that, on the rare occasions I was given a game, I made silly mistakes because I was too stressed out trying to act like a 'professional'. Then the coaches believe you played like shit because you're not switched on and aren't taking football seriously enough, and they tell you that. And that cycle continues.

I have carried this negative feedback loop with me my entire career. I am not so blind as to not recognise there were times I could have applied myself more. I guess my point is that I was young and these situations sprouted insecurities I didn't know existed. Over several years, these insecurities grew and any confidence and desire

I might have harboured to one day become Australia's first-choice keeper waned. I knew my place within the national team. A game here and there whenever Lyds was injured or needed a rest, and a support person the rest of the time. I also got to hang out with my best friends in camp a few times a year – as long as it wasn't so often that the coaches saw this smart-arse nobody fraternising with the stars of the show. It was difficult to be with Lans and Cait and Sam and Emily on game day anyway. It was the same the following day, because they only had to do recovery and I had to train with the squad members who played few to no minutes.

All of these things combined sent me inward, navel-gazing when I should have been concentrating and quiet when I should have been loud. That was literally the problem in my earlier years with the Matildas – my biggest critique was not talking enough on the field. A goalkeeper is supposed to be assertive and lead the team from the back. That requires clear, loud and direct communication. These days, I have embraced that because it's a central part of my job. Back then, though, I despised having to tell anyone what to do. To be that commanding character. Bubs was a natural at it. When she was on the field, players couldn't hear themselves think because she was in their ears non-stop. Then I'd be put in goal and wouldn't say boo. I would shout something and think, 'Oh my God, that sounded so weird.' It was cringey. I was scared of saying the wrong thing too, because I wasn't confident in my own ability. So I would second-guess my directives to outfield players.

That also led to a lot of mistakes, because I would order them to do the wrong thing or tell them to do the right thing too late. Miscommunications are responsible for so much of what goes awry in a football match. Being decisive as a goalkeeper is critical. It was a weakness of mine, for sure. But it also confused the hell out of me. The coaches wanted me to be this big voice and big presence on the field, but off it they didn't want me to socialise with the very people who had that presence.

ALANNA KENNEDY

Mac is just a really fun person. She goes with the flow and never misses a beat. What I mean is she would always get FOMO. She's a little bit different now we're a little bit older but until recently she always wanted to hang out – 'Let's do this, let's do that.' She'd always be in one of our rooms. Not in an annoying way, because she's so fun, and I hated the trips she wasn't there for. But it was just funny – whenever anyone would go somewhere, Mac would always be there. She needed to be in on the fun. Her role as a goalkeeper was different from us outfield players, because there's that hierarchy. If you're not no. 1, you're probably not going to play and are a little bit along for the ride. Sometimes, especially when we were younger, it felt as if she was pretty happy just being along for the ride; that she was more excited to travel the world with her mates than she was about the football. Don't take that in the wrong way, because it was similar for all of us at different points.

Comments would fly around from the coaching staff. For instance, if we were off to recovery and she was heading to the bus to go to training but lingered around chatting with us, it was frowned on.

I could see the frustration with both sides. Her perspective was that she would be present on the training pitch when she was genuinely needed but until she was on the training pitch, she would be with her friends. From a coaching point of view, particularly when you're younger, some of them are trying to teach us that professionalism. That can go one of two ways and I think she tended to get frustrated rather than sometimes accepting it. And I could see the frustration. She's got a bit about her, Macca – and when certain things annoyed her, she would maybe retaliate or make a little comment. I love that about her. It's probably one of the reasons we get along – she doesn't take shit. But sometimes it got her into trouble or was taken the wrong way.

8.
Parity

When I was younger, I hardly knew the names of any past Matildas, let alone the significance of the sacrifices they made so my generation could have it a little easier. I understood things on a surface level. I noticed, during my first camp at 18 years old, that somebody else set out my kit for me every day before training, then I would throw it in the wash afterwards and it would magically reappear sparkling clean before the following day's practice. Previous players not only did their own washing but also sewed their own patches onto their shirts. I came to learn all of that and more later, when I was more mature and expressed an interest and some of the older heads in the team relayed their stories.

I carried this information with me when, hours before I was due to fly from Brisbane to Canberra and then to the US for a pretty high-profile friendly tour, the players' union rang me to let me know I would actually be flying to Sydney instead. During this period, a large chunk of the team was already in the States playing in the NWSL between W-League seasons, but Professional Footballers Australia (PFA) had booked flights to Sydney for all the players based in other Australian states. The directive was to march together on FFA's offices, to request a resolution of our collective bargaining negotiations, but to still bring our suitcases with a view to flying abroad as planned if the pay negotiations were settled in time. I was 21 years old at the time, with zero interest in how the world operated outside of my bubble and a rudimentary-at-best comprehension of FFA's pay structure for the women's national team. My main thought was, 'Right, who the fuck am I about to piss off? Am I going to get dropped because of this?'

It was hard being in that position and not knowing what the consequences would be. I was a young, non-starting player who didn't want to do anything wrong by either side, but also didn't know *what* was right and wrong. If I was the player I am now, I would have done what I did 100 times over. Back then, I just did what I was told and took a backseat when it came to the important stuff. The basics in my mind were that we were trying to get more pay and FFA was being shit about it. I had no involvement in what went on in the background but it was clear I was meant to be interested. So, on 8 September 2015, off I went to Sydney with my suitcase and met up with the locally based girls in the CBD, near FFA headquarters.

I now, of course, know that the situation was as follows. A basic annual Matildas contract, which most of us were on, was $21,000 a year. That was two-thirds of the minimum wage and about a tenth of what Socceroos players earned in a year if they played all fixtures. Club contracts were considerably less than this and many players worked a second job on top of football just to make ends meet. The previous collective bargaining agreement (CBA) had been negotiated on the basis that the expected level of commitment was that of a semi-professional player, yet we had all been required to undertake a six-month World Cup preparation programme in the first half of 2016 without any adjustment to remuneration and conditions. That meant players, if they wanted to even have a chance to be selected to represent their country at a World Cup, were forced to forgo employment and family commitments with no additional compensation from FFA.

That CBA expired while we were in Canada. We had just gone deeper into a World Cup than any Matildas or Socceroos side had before and had finally broken into the Australian mainstream consciousness. Players were appearing on prime-time TV and being recognised for what we had achieved and yet each player received a grand total of $750 for playing in that quarter-final. Soon after we returned home, months-long negotiations to finalise a new CBA broke down. A couple of months after that, the matter had blown up into a full-scale industrial dispute. The players' association had tabled an offer around a two-tiered system, which would see 14 Tier 1 players earn around $40,000 a year and six Tier 2 players earn around $33,000 a year. FFA rejected the proposals as unaffordable and instead offered an increase of about 10 per cent a year over a four-year term.

In cold-hard cash, that looked like an initial rise from $21,000 to $23,000.

We were about to board a plane overseas with no CBA in place and having been paid nothing for two months.

'At this stage, we didn't have any contracts in place and we didn't know what the next steps were,' Lyds wrote for the PFA's website in 2021. 'They were asking us to go on this trip and then come back and negotiate some more contract options. For us, the most important thing wasn't the money, it was everything else that comes with it. What happens if someone gets hurt? What does insurance look like? How are we going to travel there? Who will we travel with? If something happens – worst-case scenario – are we covered?'

Lyds spoke to the media that day in Hyde Park, to announce that we had decided to strike. She was the right person to do it, being our only member of the PFA Committee in Australia at the time and she had also been to some of the CBA negotiations. The slightly humorous element was that we were all made to stand just a fraction behind her and maintain very serious facial expressions. The reality for me and a couple of other younger players, such as Larissa Crummer, was that it all just felt so weird. There we were, walking through Hyde Park in our civvies, with our suitcases, wondering if we were going to go into camp or go home. And on top of that, I had my fucking hair out, which goes to show how much I've changed. The other thing was that the coaches hadn't been told, so Staj and Jonesy and all the other staff were waiting for us at the AIS.

I think all of our phones rang at some stage, presumably after FFA had broken the news to them, but nobody else was answering so I toed the line on that, too.

The tour had sold 60,000 tickets for the two friendlies and we didn't show up. But we had the support of the American girls and even Hope Solo tweeted her support, which was a proud goalkeepers' union moment.

'The players made a decision that some sort of action needed to occur to get FFA's attention and let them know we were serious and the players' expectation was much higher,' Kate Gill, who was in that squad and is now a PFA co-chief executive, said in 2023. 'It was a watershed moment for the players and the players to come, and women's sport in general. Off the back of that, the A-League Women's competition started to take flight and we were able to bargain that, AFLW started and cricket has always been a leader in how they treated their female players. The domestic sports in Australia really took off. I felt like the Matildas' moment created that opportunity.'

We were the first – and only – national sporting team to go on strike in the modern era. And it worked – our maximum salary jumped to $41,000. Four years later, in 2019, a new CBA ensured Australia became the first country in which its female national team players earn the same pay as the men and share the revenue from ticket sales and broadcast deals. In the long run, these advancements probably benefited FFA, in that they would have helped the new Football Australia administration win hosting rights for the 2023 World Cup. In that tournament, a squad of players received $138,000 in prizemoney for making the quarter-finals (184 times what we got for making the same stage in 2015) and $253,000 for making the semis. On the eve of the tournament, the PFA released a video recorded by all 23 of us in the World Cup squad. In it, we stood up for rival nations who are still denied the basic right of collective bargaining for their wages and working conditions, and had a crack at FIFA for still only offering women one-quarter as much prize money as men for the same achievements.

Early in October 2015, once the team had collectively accepted an interim CBA deal, we committed to a tour of China scheduled for later that same month. In Chongqing, I played the first friendly, a 1–1 draw with China, and Lyds played in the 1–0 loss to England. It was my eighth cap and, while this isn't a big number, most had come within the past year under Staj. He was still playing me in whatever the lesser fixture was of each international window and continued that pattern for our 2016 Olympic qualifiers in Japan the following March. Of our five matches, I played in our 9–0 win over Vietnam and then, after our qualification had been confirmed, our final 1–1 draw with China. That June, I played in an Olympic warm-up friendly, a 2–0 win over New Zealand in Ballarat. Lyds then played in the 1–1 rematch in Melbourne. The Ballarat game was interesting in that I started and then Staj gave Casey some minutes towards the end of the match. I played really well and got applauded as I was substituted off.

It was an odd feeling to enjoy it, given how my internal monologue usually operated. While I wanted to play, the notion of actually doing so was increasingly feeling like less of an opportunity and more of a chance for me to screw up. If I was named in the XI the night before a game, the next 24 hours were spent hoping and bargaining with invisible gods and offering up almost anything just to get me through it unscathed. I would be full of nerves the second I woke up and actually pictured myself making error after error. This continued throughout the day; when the match finally started, I counted down the minutes until it was over. All of that aside, I was selected as one of the two goalkeepers in the 18-player Olympic squad.

I don't know if it's because I knew Lydia was still the first choice and that she deserved to be there – her 2015 World Cup had been exceptional – but this period of my Matildas career is not particularly memorable. Again, I had a feeling I might get to play what was perceived as our easiest fixture and, again, I did play. This time, it was our final group game against Zimbabwe. We had to win to progress, because we had lost our opener 2–0 to Canada and then drawn 2–2 with Germany in São Paulo, and we needed to retain our spot in the group to ensure we'd go through as one of the best third-placed teams. We defeated Zimbabwe 6–1 with little fuss. Ellie Carpenter came on in the final 15 minutes and became the youngest footballer to take part in the Olympics. It's crazy to think she was in Year 10 at school and had only turned 16 three months prior, having made her senior international debut that March as a 15-year-old. Personally, having got my job out of the way and joined Ellie in officially becoming an Olympian, I was just content to watch the rest of the tournament from the bench.

But Brazil put on a good show and it was cool having Mum and Dad there for all the games, travelling around the country with the other parents. The Olympic Village was a lot of fun, too, and great for celebrity-spotting. In the end, we had to play the host nation in the quarter-finals in Belo Horizonte. The raucous crowd at the 52,000-capacity Mineirão was wild. Football in Brazil is as important as religion and its people's commitment to the women's game was just as strong from where I was sitting.

PAUL JONES

A couple of days before the quarter-final against Brazil, I had a discussion with Staj about maybe bringing Mackenzie on if the game looked like going to penalties. Even back then, she was a sensational penalty-stopper, to the point that during Matildas penalty practice before the 2015 World Cup, I had to tell her not to try so hard to stop them because the girls needed to actually score some to help with their confidence. Staj said that he would think about bringing Mackenzie on if and when penalties came into play. As it panned out, Staj had to use his last substitution to bring on Larissa Crummer in extra time, so there was no decision to be made. Add to this that Lydia saved a shot from Marta in the 119th minute, which I don't think Mackenzie would have made, and then put us in a position to win the shootout when she saved Marta's penalty. Unfortunately, we missed our next penalty – and two more kicks later, our tournament was over.

I know objectively that what occurred in this match was heartbreaking for us. I can relay bits of info, like that it was still 0–0 at the end of extra time and went to penalties. That, during one of the longer penalty shootouts in history, Brazil's goalkeeper Bárbara repeatedly came off her line illegally and was not pulled up for it. And that, because of this, Lans had to step up as our eighth penalty-taker and had to score to keep us in it. When she didn't, I just remember her head dropping into her hands. It was an awful moment for her. But the reality was she didn't lose that game for us. The next day, Sam told the media she thought the parochial crowd may have had 'a little bit of an impact' on the referee, who could have been afraid to upset the spectators by sanctioning Bárbara for breaking the rules. She explained to them, 'On the bench, we noticed the first one but we obviously scored it. We thought if she missed, they would have retaken it but it wasn't the case on the last one.'

Elise Kellond-Knight also spoke about some potential pre-match antics from Brazilian police, who kept our team bus waiting an extra 10 minutes before allowing us to travel to the stadium. 'Even before the match, we had a delay getting out of the hotel and you just question Brazilian police looking after us, what's really going on,' she said. 'It's just little games like this. The Brazilian bus took off and we sat in the car park for a little bit, thinking, "What's happening?" It puts your preparation out a little bit when you're on a tight schedule.'

It was obviously sad we didn't make the semi-finals, in which we would have faced Sweden (who eventually lost the gold-medal match to Germany). But the fact I was hardly playing made it feel like I had little emotional attachment to our results. I wanted the girls to do well and be happy, but I strangely didn't actually feel much either way.

My detachment continued when I returned to Queensland and signed with Brisbane Roar. It's the only reason I can think to explain why I gave serious consideration to playing in the inaugural AFLW season. I had been introduced to Australian rules footy in 2015, after the World Cup and before I began my second Perth Glory season. I was back at home for five or six weeks so trained with the Roar. Queensland AFLW club Coorparoo was down some players so asked if any of us wanted to come down and play. Myself, Amy Chapman and Larissa thought we might as well. I was still at the stage where I wasn't sure if football would work out and figured a bit of extra fitness wouldn't hurt. I played full forward and loved it so much I played for the rest of the season until I had to get back to the W-League.

I had never played before, being from Queensland and from a rugby league family. But playing footy with my brother when growing up meant I could both kick and catch a ball of that shape, and it turned out that was basically all I needed to know. There were some rules I wasn't up to speed on and it took me a while to start handballing instead of just throwing. But I just picked it up as I went. A part of me worried that I might injure myself right before the season but I escaped with nothing more than a couple of jarred fingers. I didn't get knocked around a lot because of my size. Poor Amy, though, got tackled and broke her collarbone. It put her out for half her pre-season. The coach of Coorparoo, former AFL player Craig Starcevich, ended up becoming coach of the Brisbane Lions. In 2016, a couple of weeks before the draft, he gauged my interest. I was definitely keen and did check over my Matildas and W-League contracts to understand how feasible it might be. It became pretty clear, pretty quickly, that it wouldn't have been possible and I had to decline.

Signing with the Roar was a novelty. Even though I had trained with Brisbane a lot when I was younger and whenever I was home, between seasons elsewhere, I had never signed with them because Casey was always the starting keeper. But poor Casey had been through a shit time with a whole chain of injuries. In 2012, it was osteitis pubis – a chronic inflammation of the pelvic region. In 2014, she suffered a lacerated liver, and in 2015, she did her ACL. Those circumstances aside, the next two years there were good for me. For the first season, I lived back at home, which was a return to normality after a few years of moving around different states. Harking back to my school days at the QAS, I drove to Brisbane every day to train and then again to play on the weekends. I also bought my first apartment that year. Mum and Dad had always encouraged me to purchase – real estate was something they were interested in and they wanted me to invest my earnings wisely.

Results-wise, the two years were very different from each other. In 2016–17, we placed seventh from nine teams and well outside the finals; in 2017–18, we finished top of the table as premiers, only to be knocked out in the semi-finals by Melbourne City. In 2017–18, I was also awarded goalkeeper of the year, for the third time, and my contract had risen to in the vicinity of $25,000. But it was just good vibes, too. Club talisman Polks was our captain and our squad also featured Katrina Gorry, Tameka Yallop, Hayley Raso, Amy Chapman and Emily Gielnik, and a very young Cortnee Vine and Kaitlyn Torpey – several years before either of their Matildas debuts. Being close to home was familiar and comforting but I was also far enough away from the Gold Coast to start properly exploring an important part of me without fear of judgement.

9.
The Talk

The media's fascination with the personal lives of gay female footballers is sort of bizarre. I have never really understood why that's the case. Hetero relationships – unless famous people are involved – rarely seem to attract the same level of interest.

I do acknowledge that the women's game possibly has the highest proportion of openly gay players in global sport, and because of that we have an important platform to help normalise the experiences of the LGBTQI+ community in everyday life. I just don't understand the intrigue factor – why the media see a lesbian couple and have to ask about their relationship. They see a goalscorer at a World Cup and must know who she's in a relationship with before they want to find out how many other goals she's scored. A part of it might be that it's still a relatively new topic of conversation, especially in Australia. There's a bit of novelty in it, perhaps. Does a stereotypical straight couple seem pretty boring when you can get a relationship with the added twist of two girls holding hands?

Having said all of that, I am proud of my sexuality and I do make some parts of my personal life public on social media. That I now feel comfortable enough in who I am to show my relationship to the world is a relief. It didn't always feel this easy. Sometimes, I forget how emotionally confusing my life used to be. I should use the plural 'lives', really, because until I was 23, I was living two of them very separately.

Throughout school, I never really thought about the possibility of being anything other than straight. Straight was all there was on the Gold Coast growing up. All of my friends were girly girls. I only knew what was in front of me: girls liked boys and boys liked girls. It never occurred to me that there could be anything outside those boxes until I started at the QAS, when I was almost 17. In that set-up, so many players were gay. And everybody was so open and honest about it. That was when I started to wonder. There wasn't really a moment I realised; I just unconsciously started thinking that the gender of the person I might like didn't matter. So when I started to find myself becoming attracted to girls, it felt natural. But only within that environment. For some reason, I didn't feel like I could be who I wanted to be on the Gold Coast. This big secret disconnected me from everyone in my original life. It's so hard to stay close with your mates when there is a blockage somewhere deep inside you that stops you from sharing your whole self with them. When every time you talk with them your guard is up, ready to steer the conversation away from anything to do with relationships or hook-ups.

My logic was that, while there was still a possibility I might end up with a guy long term, it felt easier to keep up the pretence to family and friends. So I lived one life in Brisbane and one life on the Gold Coast, and each side of the divide knew next to nothing about the other. I posted nothing on social media that would offer any clues and divulged no information in any other way. Of course, my friends from school asked questions anyway. In their eyes, I hadn't been in a relationship for ages. They were wondering if I was ever going to get with someone, curious about who I was spending time with while I was away in my football world. I know now that my friends wouldn't have cared – and they said that at the time. Yet I would still insist that I would never go there, tell them not to be stupid. I was adamant I would not tell a soul. After six years, the split-identity façade just got too exhausting. In 2017, after the break-up of a two-year relationship, I told my best schoolfriend, Shaquille.

SHAQUILLE BOND

I remember the night vividly. Kenz had been back home but I hadn't really seen her much at all. Then she just randomly called me on a weeknight – she was bawling her eyes out. She asked if she could come over, said she needed to see me in person. I said of course. When she arrived, she was still crying – and Kenz doesn't cry; she's not an emotional person at all. But she was so upset that, initially,

I thought someone had died. Then I thought she'd had a massive fight with her mum. It took her a while to calm down enough to get it out. Eventually, she said, 'I'm in a relationship.' I was like, 'Okay, and?' Then she said, 'I have a girlfriend.' Still, I was thinking, 'And why are you upset?' because, in my head, it was something bigger. Once her emotions settled down a bit, she told me she had been seeing this girl in Brisbane, where she was playing with the Roar, and she had been a little bit more distant with us because she didn't know how to be both people at once.

She ended up telling me because something had happened with her girlfriend at that time that meant the relationship had ended. I think that's why she was doubly upset: she wanted to tell me about this shit thing that had happened to her but to tell me she had to also tell me that she was in a relationship with a girl. She said she had been hiding this whole other life, that she was out in Brisbane, going to gay bars and being a completely different person to what we knew, and she didn't know how to tell us. I said, 'Firstly, I'm not surprised. I mean, you're the biggest tomboy I know, so it's not as if it's a complete shock. Secondly, I couldn't care less. It doesn't matter if you like girls or boys, it doesn't change anything.' It just makes me sad that she didn't feel like she could tell me earlier. But at the same time, I can't even imagine what that would have been like. She had grown up saying she liked boys and even at this point didn't tell me she was a lesbian – she said she was bi but that she was done with girls and wouldn't be with a girl again. I just rolled with it, but suggested we tell our friend Liv together so she knew there was nothing to be worried about.

I think that was also a relief for Kenz. A little while after that, she opened up to the rest of our friend group about being gay, and everyone was so supportive and happy for her. However, I am really grateful she was playing soccer, because it meant she was surrounded by a lot more people in the gay community who were able to help her from their personal experience. Although we all loved and supported her no matter what, at the time it was a very foreign thing to be openly out (on the Gold Coast), so I can't even imagine how that would have felt for her.

During school – and this will sound bad now, but please keep in mind it was 13 years ago and the world was a lot less politically correct – we both used to call each other 'lesbian' as a joke. Kenz and I were often called that by others, too, because we played soccer and basketball, which were not your stereotypical 'girly' sports. Kenz had definitely dated boys, but if I'm being honest she would usually show more interest in feminine or 'pretty' guys, and we would always joke that she was the boy when she was seeing guys. Since her coming out and seeing how she is in a relationship with a girl, it's so obvious how much more herself and comfortable she is.

Shaquille was so reassuring. She is a beautiful friend and I am still very close with her and her family today. Even then, though, I still didn't want to come out to my family. That was partly because I was convinced at the time that I was done with girls – I actually started dating a guy not long after that, although it lasted only a couple of months. By the time I had talked with Shaquille, many of the Matildas girls were already out. They encouraged me to tell my family. I said there was no way I was going to do that. I was terrified.

But as it looked more and more likely I might actually end up with a girl, I started to think about it a little more seriously. My sneaking around had created a chasm between Mum and me. I had spent years telling the kinds of lies you concoct as a teenager when you don't want your parents to know you're doing something naughty. I was in my early 20s and here I was pretending I was staying at Mini's when I wanted to see my girlfriend in Brisbane.

In the end, it came out by chance. It was 2017, not long before that year's Tournament of Nations, and I was back at home and moping around the house a bit. The break-up was still fresh but I had been okay until this point because I'd been travelling and busy. As soon as I got back to the Gold Coast, the memories flooded back in. Mum sat me down and asked me what was wrong. My head told me to say nothing but my heart wanted to feel closer to her. After some gentle prodding, I could feel the words forming almost against my will. I told her she would be disappointed hearing what I was about to say. She asked me outright if I had been with a girl. I told her we had just split up.

Shortly afterwards I left, bound for the Tournament of Nations in the US, feeling raw about my semi-accidental decision to come out.

In camp, life at least felt a bit more normal and it was easy to get swept up in the pomp of American sport. This was a friendly tournament but the publicity around it was ridiculous and the crowds were next level. Women's football in the States was a decade ahead of the rest of the world. The players were like celebrities. It was so far removed from anything I had ever experienced. And can you imagine what happened? We beat the US in Seattle, in the first of our three round-robin games. Lyds started, Tameka scored and we won 1–0. To this day, it remains the only time we have ever beaten America. We did that while they were at the peak of their powers, too. It got us up and away to take out the tournament. I played in the second and third matches – a 4–2 win over world no. 6 Japan in San Diego and a 6–1 rout of world no. 8 Brazil in Los Angeles. It was one of my first times playing against a team inside the top 10. It was part of a seven-game winning streak that propelled us from a seventh world ranking at the start of the tournament to fourth in mid-December. Results aside, I knew I had played well. And I didn't want to leave that feeling behind. That meant not heading back to Australia right away, so I tagged along with Cait on a holiday in the States for a couple of days, then went with her to Japan, where she and Mini were playing and living in Sendai.

CAITLIN FOORD

It was like when I was in Perth, going through a difficult time, but this time the shoe was on the other foot. Macca came to stay with Mini, me and an American who was living with us at the time. I asked my team in Japan if Mac could come and train with us. I wanted to be there for her and just get her away from what she was struggling with. We honestly had the best time. It was so much fun and she got a taste of what an international environment was like, training with a team overseas and just being in a different culture. She had obviously been away with the national team but it's different when you live in a place compared to staying in a hotel and having everything looked after for you. We were on a high after winning the Tournament of Nations and Macca was able to ride that high with us in Japan, which probably wouldn't have happened had she gone home.

After the visit, I headed for Tokyo. I remember walking around the city, feeling restless, upset, lost. I had a sudden impulse to confide in my brother. Sam and I weren't all that close at that point and I'm not entirely sure what made me send the text. But I typed: 'I need to talk to you.'

Sam: 'What's up? Do you want to call?'

Me: 'I should probably call but I'll start crying. I know you pretty much know anyway but I wanted to tell you before you find out another way. I had a girlfriend for the past couple of years. We broke up a couple of months ago, though, and that's been the last of it. I'm sorry if you're disappointed.'

Sam: 'Kenzo, I have your back 100%. It doesn't matter if you have gay feelings or you don't. You must go with your heart and what makes you happy. You don't have to justify yourself. The only thing is, I'm disappointed for you not telling me this two years ago. I would have wanted to meet her, etc., but I must say I'm sorry if I haven't exactly made myself approachable to talk to me about it. I'm really glad you've told me about it now and you can talk to me about it whenever you like . . . I love you very much and always will.'

Me: 'Well, I didn't know how to tell you and I didn't want to make a big deal out of something that I'm not even sure about myself. But you did meet her, she came out with us one night . . . I wanted to tell you that night but still wasn't sure how. Thank you for that message, though. I know Mum is probably hurt by it but I don't want her thinking different of me 'cause nothing's changed, you know. It's just so hard to try to figure out by myself.'

Sam: 'Haha, it's called bi-curious – there's nothing to figure out. If you're attracted to both sexes then no biggie, it's just a sex. It just comes down to the particular person, if you like them or not, regardless of their sex.'

I still struggle to read this conversation without crying. It was just such a big emotional release; it was also new for Sam and me to talk about feelings with each other. I think that's why we changed the subject pretty quickly after that to something random like tattoos. It was a bit 'oh gosh, we're getting deep here'.

My dad didn't really have too much to say about it – he's a pretty quiet guy who just goes with the flow. But when you get him one on one, especially after he's had a couple of drinks and gets comfortable, he's hilarious. On the whole, he just wants everyone to be happy. My current partner, Kirsty, met my family during the World Cup. A few months later, Kirsty spent Christmas with all of us at our family home and it was very much a family acknowledging us as a couple. My parents bought Kirsty a Christmas present, and then another for her 30th birthday. The more comfortable I felt in my own skin, the less I would try to hide my sexual orientation.

10.
Changes

Breaking into the national team was becoming more and more important to me. Not in the sense that I wanted to displace Lyds – we got along with each other so well and were kindred spirits of sorts, because we had lived and trained together in Canberra, and to this day we've always had each other's backs. I just wanted to be ready whenever my time came and to ensure I wasn't leap-frogged by anyone younger and less experienced. Every decision (Aussie rules foray aside) was made with that in mind – and the next logical step was to play club football overseas. I needed more games at a higher level, with more at stake. The world's top league at the time was the NWSL. It made sense to follow in the footsteps of my higher-profile national teammates, who played in the US and then in the off-season returned to Australia and played W-League. But my lack of Matildas caps meant I had no reputation off which to get a contract offer in the States. Lydia had played in Sweden for a bit before she went to the NWSL.

My agent at the time got me a spot with top-flight Norwegian club Arna-Bjørnar.

It was a great move for me at the time. In the W-League, I could get away with anything because I was starting every week anyway and the quality wasn't as high. Then you go to European football and they're a lot more serious and you really need to be on your game. Football aside, I grew a lot off the field as well. I didn't always enjoy it but living overseas forced me out of my comfort zone. And to be honest, I think I needed it.

SAM ARNOLD

Mum always preferred to handle Kenz's money. When she was younger, that was a really good thing, because Kenz wasn't able to spend what she earned on clothes and other things; it was all invested into something that would benefit her in the long term. And Mum always ensured she never wanted for anything in day-to-day life. Couple that with the fact that everything else was done for Kenz by whichever club she played for – living arrangements, laundry, the trash taken out, the whole lot – and the logistics of her life were completely removed from most people's reality. She got her very first taste of real independence when she moved overseas. Even then, rent and everything else was subsidised. But at least she was getting her fingers a little dirty handling utility bills and things like that.

I came into my own while living in Bergen. I knew no one in the team and they were all from the city so all had their own lives. They came to training, then went to work at their other jobs or went home. My teammates were all so lovely and I got along well with them all, but they understandably weren't going to jump at the chance to hang out with a foreigner who didn't speak a word of their native language. As it turned out, I didn't mind my own company and relished having my own space in my flat. Almost as soon as I came to this realisation, an American joined the team and moved in with me. Her name was Jamia Fields and she had signed from Orlando Pride, where she had played alongside my Matildas teammates Steph Catley, Laura Alleway (now Brock) and Lisa De Vanna, and other Americans, including Alex Morgan. The place was a bit cramped for the both of us and it took away that independence I was starting to enjoy. But Jamia made me laugh and we got on well. By the time she left, about halfway through the season, we'd become good friends.

The 2023 World Cup quarter-final was not my first penalty shootout experience at an international tournament. That was five years earlier, in Jordan, where we were contesting the 2018 Asian Cup. It was April and I was getting close to becoming a starter. I could feel it. Once more, I started our easiest group game – an 8–0 win over Vietnam – and Lydia sandwiched that with a 0–0 draw with South Korea and a 1–1 draw with Japan. Combined, the results ensured we topped Group B and cruised through to the semi-finals, in which we were to face Thailand.

PAUL JONES

We were pretty happy to get Thailand because we had hammered them 5–0 just the previous month in Perth. Staj and I decided to start Mackenzie as a means of exposing her to a big knockout game, reasoning that we should win it comfortably. Everybody else also clearly thought we should win easily and that manifested as complacency. Almost everyone played poorly and that did not exclude Mackenzie. She just wasn't focused, making a couple of errors that cost us goals and put us on the back foot. It took an injury-time 2–2 equaliser from Alanna to send the game into extra time. Well, once we had survived the next 30 minutes, I stopped worrying, because I knew what Mackenzie could do with penalties. And even though the pressure was on to remedy her earlier mistakes, she stood tall and saved three consecutive spot kicks before Sam converted the one to win it for us.

Can you make up for a shit game by winning the subsequent penalty shootout? Not in my mind. I was devastated. Things had been going well and I could see Staj was beginning to have faith in me. I know Thailand were ranked 30th, compared to our fourth, but it was still a semi-final. I played like shit, made mistakes I didn't usually make, like miskicking balls to our opponents. We won in the end and my performance during the actual match was forgotten by everyone – except me. The girls buzzed excitedly around me and started looking towards the final but I just couldn't bring myself to celebrate under the circumstances. Staj must have noticed it, because he texted me the next morning and asked me to see him in our meeting room.

When I arrived and we sat down, he simply asked, 'How are you feeling?' That was enough. I broke down and told him everything. That I had felt like I was so close and that now I had ruined my chances.

He let me talk, then told me this didn't change anything – yes, I made some mistakes but it wouldn't define me as a goalkeeper. It was the first conversation of that kind I had ever had with Staj – the moment I realised how much he cared about us as both players and as people. Sometimes, because of the old-school way he approaches his coaching, players thought he was a bit of a prick. And he was certainly competitive – he wanted to win every game. That could feel intimidating. Meanwhile, I was so stressed about what he thought of me that I found it hard to form a connection. All that changed during this meeting; he showed me he was in my corner and wanted the best for me, and that motivated me to want to be better.

ALEN STAJCIC, coach

That was a pivotal moment, for me and for Macca. I had played her because I wanted to see if she could step up at that level. When I started with the Matildas, the second and third goalkeepers had almost no caps under their belts, so I tried to give them all as much as I could. This was a big moment for her and she basically cost us a couple of goals in that game, and it went down to the wire. She got chipped for the first goal, which was only half her fault, but with the second goal, she shanked the ball straight to their striker and they scored and ended up leading 2–1 until the last minute. But Macca is brilliant at penalties – she's the best women's player

Australia has ever had on penalties. She ended up winning the day for the team.

Internally, she had thought that that was it for her, that she'd had her chance and ruined it. The conversation revolved around the fact I didn't think that at all. That if I didn't believe in her, I wouldn't have played her in a semi-final. That this was just a part of her learning and growing. She broke down and started crying, and said that was all she wanted – to know she was still a chance.

I always told her she had the tools to be better than what she was and to challenge Lydia for the no. 1 spot. At that time, Lydia had more attributes that were better than her but, certainly, there were lots of things in Macca's game that I thought should make her better than Lydia. They just hadn't really come to the surface consistently. Whether it was dedication, focus, experience, age – or a combination of those things – she went into games just hoping she'd have a good game. For a goalkeeper, more than any other position, you have to be concentrating in the moment all the time, because the consequences are so much bigger. One error there and it's much more costly than if a striker makes a mistake. So it was like, 'Okay, you didn't have your best game but you still won us the game. Take the positives away but learn from it and start bringing out all the other stuff.'

Had Staj not instigated that conversation, I probably would have spiralled, but he helped me frame it so that it didn't feel like the end of the world. It just goes to show how a few words from someone you respect can change a lot for you. There would be another couple of similar interactions with other mentors over the years, which have stayed with me in a similar way.

The morning after that, I received a phone call from Mum to let me know my nana – Dad's mum – had passed. I had never really experienced a loss in my family before. My pop had died from leukaemia when I was very young – I didn't remember him enough to miss his effect on my family. So this news hit me pretty hard. I was distraught and called Dad to check on him. Dad and I don't really do serious with each other. We're best friends but in the sense that we muck around. The fact I was crying to him was unusual. He was at work when he picked up the phone and said he was okay, but then I heard his voice break and he quickly said he had to go. Because Dad never cries. He's your typical father from that generation who fixes everything and doesn't let others see his emotions. That was when I realised – 'Holy shit, he's just lost his mum.' That gave me yet another perspective on our Asian Cup campaign. I simply checked out. All I could think about was that Dad had to say goodbye to his mum. I kept tearing up just trying to imagine how that would feel for me. The coaches were really good about it. They pulled me in and hugged me, and made sure I was okay. They understood why I was the way I was but it was fucking hard. Lyds played the final and we lost 1–0 to Japan.

I played seven games for the Matildas over the course of 2018, which was more than any other year to date. It included the full 90 of our away friendlies against France and England, and a 5–0 friendly win over Chile in Newcastle. Staj had put me on a Tier 1 contract, which was encouraging. But then something happened that threw everything out of whack.

On 19 January 2019, Staj was sacked. Behind the scenes, I still don't know exactly what happened and how it all unfolded, only that I received a phone call from the PFA asking if I had ever been bullied by staff or was made to feel uncomfortable. The answer was no, I had not. My assumption was that there must have been some other players who did report feeling that way. All I knew was that I had progressed so much under Staj, had earned my respect from him and felt that he believed in me. Now I had to start all over again with somebody else. Jonesy left at the same time. I sent a message to both to thank them for everything they had done. I specifically made sure Staj knew that I appreciated everything and I didn't know what was going on for this to happen. I wanted him to know it wasn't all of us who felt that way. Staj was maybe one of the hardest coaches I've ever had but I personally felt like he cared about me the most.

It was a pretty stressful time for the team, especially being six months out from the 2019 World Cup. Of course, I was so focused on how it might affect my chances of being selected for that tournament in France that a lot of the media mayhem passed me by. The one thing I do remember clearly was Caitlin crashing her car into a taxi as we arrived together at the Crowne Plaza in Coogee and all the waiting cameras filming the whole thing.

About a month later, Ante Milicic was appointed to replace Staj until the end of the World Cup. I only knew what I read about Ante: that he was a former Socceroos assistant with a wealth of experience in the men's game but none in the women's. I didn't care about that and I don't think anyone else did either. The most noticeable thing when Ante arrived was how everybody was suddenly out of their comfort zone. Many of the Matildas had come from NSW so had grown up with Staj; us Queensland girls had been involved with him in some way or another from pretty early on as well. Staj was a sort of safety net – we all knew where we stood and how he operated. Ante was an unknown quantity and that made us all feel that we needed to step up. He wasn't intimidating but he knew his shit, and he was quite serious. You could hear in his voice he wasn't someone you wanted to cross. Any fears we had about finding a pair of capable hands in time for the World Cup were allayed after our very first camp. We realised after a while that Ante had a softer side to him, too. We just had to pick and choose when the mood was right to banter.

Whatever I did or didn't do clearly didn't work, because Ante played me in his second match in charge – a 4–1 Cup of Nations win over South Korea in Brisbane – and then once more a year later – a 6–0 Tokyo Olympics-qualifying defeat of, you guessed it, Thailand – and that was it. I was in the 23-player World Cup squad and went to France but didn't get a single minute.

The apparent problem with my choice of friends had also transferred to the minds of the new coaching staff. During one of the camps, Ante's assistant, Ivan Jolić, asked to speak with me. They hadn't yet redone all the contracts – the Tier 1 contract Staj had put me on wasn't really heard of for a back-up goalkeeper. Anyway, Ivan said something along the lines of, 'I saw you're on a Tier 1 . . . do you deserve to be on a Tier 1?' 'Here we go,' I thought. I told him I thought I was on the cusp of break-ing into the team and had played some good games. I don't believe he was trying to be rude, just genuinely asking. But then he made the comment that I seemed to hang out with the big dogs of the team. I told him I didn't hang out with them because they were big dogs; I hung out with them because we'd been best friends since we were 15 or 16 years old. 'But you sit at the head of the table with all the big dogs and you're not really a big dog yet,' he said. He was referring to the table in our meal room. Generally, when you arrive in camp and sit down for your first meal, you end up returning to that same seat for the duration of the stay. It isn't a planned thing; it's just that players tend to gravitate back to where they started. This particu-lar meal room had long tables instead of circular ones and we happened to be at the end of the 'head' of one of them. That comment from Ivan is exactly the sort of shit I can-not stand. I hate being portrayed as somebody who thinks they're better than they are, because the opposite was true of my personality – my problem was that I never believed I was good enough. But here we were, going through the same thing all over again. So I made a point of sitting away from Lans and Cait and the girls I was closest to for the sole purpose of trying not to appear better than what

I was. The girls tried to tell me not to worry but they didn't understand that their status as regular starters meant they had the luxury of being able to do that. Ivan did say he understood what I was saying and that it was okay – that he was just pointing out the optics. But I never wanted to give them an excuse to form this perception again.

11.

West Ham

The only thing I remember about that Olympic qualifier against Thailand is that it was supposed to be played
in China. Wuhan, to be exact. Yes, *that* Wuhan. We
were in pre-camp in Sydney in February of 2020 when
the COVID-19 coverage started to really ramp up. As
we were all watching the news, it became apparent that
ground zero was the host of the Asian Olympic qualifiers.
I wouldn't say we were panicking but there were definitely a few profanity-punctuated enquiries flying around.
Our team doctor was being peppered with questions and
calmly told us all would be fine. As we now know, all
was not fine. FA moved pretty quickly to host the tournament in Australia. After that, we had two play-offs against
Vietnam, the first leg in Sydney and the second in Cẩm
Phả. When we arrived for the away leg, we were asked
to wear face masks – a concept completely foreign to us
at the time. We had no idea how necessary they would
become.

Pretty soon after that, Australia had effectively cut itself off from the rest of the world and I was stranded at home, having just finished another season with Brisbane after returning from Norway. Football had stopped all over the world. There was nothing much to do but hang about and try to keep fit until it was safe to return to work again. While this time was obviously very distressing for a lot of people internationally, the sitting still gave me time to ponder my next move. Ante was still keeping us all on our toes and the by-product of that was each of us trying to sign for the right clubs to bring our games up a level.

The tournament opened with our 2–1 loss to Italy, who were ranked 15th, compared to our sixth at the time, and widely viewed as inferior. The truth was, Italy had been investing heavily in women's football, especially at big clubs like Juventus, and almost all of their national team members played in the highly regarded Serie A league. Of the 24 teams contesting the 2019 World Cup, the States were the only non-European nation to make the quarter-finals. The landscape was changing fast and we had to hustle to keep up or risk slipping down the pecking order.

I was one of the few Aussie girls who had played in Europe but Norway's Toppserien wasn't considered one of the big leagues in the way that the English Women's Super League, France's Division 1 Féminine and Spain's Liga F were. The subsequent 12 months turned into a mass exodus from the W-League/NWSL merry-go-round, as teammates had their agents put out feelers for attractive suitors who would not only offer continental and cup football on top of regular leagues but also pay players (far more) to stay contracted year-round. In other words, make women fully professional. Sam was the first major move when she signed with Chelsea in November 2019. In early 2020, Cait joined Arsenal and was followed a few months later by Steph and Lyds, and it sort of went from there. Hayley Raso went to Everton (and then Manchester City and Real Madrid) and Ellie joined perennial French champions Lyon.

I don't remember Ante saying it point blank but the inference was definitely that all the better players were doing it – I figured I could increase my chances of playing by doing it, too. I already knew I wanted to go to the UK's Women's Super League (WSL) – Cait and Sam had offered glowing reviews. My situation was a bit of a catch-22, though, because to get a visa you had to have a certain number of points accrued from appearances with your national team. I knew that would make it tricky for me, so my family helped me look into obtaining a different class of visa, on the grounds that my grandfather was born in Manchester. I stayed in touch with my agent all through that time and initially had an offer from Reading, who were up in the WSL and doing quite well. I was stoked with that and pretty much ready to accept it. I was talking it over with my family at our holiday house near Coffs Harbour, where my mum, brother and I spent quite a bit of time during COVID and made some really nice memories. I was sitting out the back when my agent called to inform me I'd had an offer from West Ham. I knew next to nothing about English football at this point but even I knew who West Ham was. It turned out my agent at the time represented another goalkeeper they had recently let go – the manager Matt Beard needed a replacement. Matt called me within 24 hours and sounded super keen. I couldn't believe it. I said absolutely and forgot about Reading almost immediately. That was in late May; by 9 July, I had my visa and travel approval, and was on a flight to London. When I arrived, they asked me who I support. In my naivety, I said Liverpool. They couldn't believe I had said it, and I didn't understand the seriousness of what it means to tie yourself to a certain club – especially when you are signing for another!

The adventure excited me to no end. I'd only ever seen London in movies – it could not have been more different to the Gold Coast. Plus Sam and Cait were already living there. I watched a couple of West Ham games from the previous season on YouTube so I had an idea of what I was coming into. I didn't exactly meet my new team in the typical way, though. Because everyone in London was still in lockdown, we had to do it all virtually on a Zoom call. It did at least break the ice before I walked in on my first day of pre-season to some pretty awkward social distancing. We all had to sit three metres apart in our indoor artificial dome, so it made making friends a little more challenging. But the banter filled the deficit. The English banter is so similar to that of Aussies and let's just say they were really speaking my language. I lived with three other girls who had also joined the team that season and snagged the biggest room upstairs with an en suite, by virtue of being the oldest in the house. Living with me were forward Nor Mustafa, a then 18-year-old from Sweden who now plays for the Syrian national team; centre-back Grace Fisk, a Brit who had joined six months earlier from Millwall; and full-back Maz Pacheco, another Brit who had moved down from Reading. I got along well with all of them, although Fisky was pretty standoffish with me at the start. She already knew Maz from the England youth teams so the pair of them hung out quite a bit. Now we laugh about that, because she ended up becoming one of my best friends in the team and we moved in together a year later.

I loved everything about London. When I first arrived, I managed to catch the back end of summer, so we enjoyed a couple of garden days in the sun and brought the TV outside to watch football. I thought the weather was pretty sweet in this part of the world. That didn't last very long at all and my Queensland constitution struggled when winter hit. That first November and December were bloody freezing but everyone kept telling me to 'wait until January' – then I'd know what cold felt like. Once January arrived and I hit my limit, they would start warning me 'just wait until February'. Well, it snowed in March. Training and playing in those conditions took some getting used to. There are times in winter when the pitch freezes a bit and becomes so hard the coaching staff push training back until later in the morning, when they can thaw it out a bit with the heaters. But the football culture makes up for the discomfort. I had never before been around that kind of fandom before, with all the chants and songs and centuries-old traditions. The earliest incarnation of the Hammers was founded in 1895 as Thames Ironworks FC, made up of the factory team from Thames Ironworks and Shipbuilding Company, the last surviving shipbuilder on the River Thames. When I arrived, I knew nothing about 'I'm Forever Blowing Bubbles', the club's famous anthem, or the novelty hammers that 1930s crowd members, decked out in trench coats and top hats, brought with them to wield during games at Upton Park.

That was, of course, the men's team. West Ham United Women was founded in 1991 and started playing in the lower divisions of the Greater London Regional Women's Football League, eventually working their way up to the Greater London League Premier Division just before the turn of the century. The girls worked their way up the pyramid until, in 2018, they successfully gained entry into the WSL. Matt was the inaugural WSL coach; since I've been there, two more have come and gone in Olli Harder and Paul Konchesky, and we've never finished higher than sixth (2021–22). We generally lose more games than we win, which the Aussie girls at highflyers Chelsea, Arsenal and Manchester City give me quite a bit of shit about. But hey, at least I've always been busy. From the start, I was starting every week and growing in confidence. All of a sudden, I was facing all these top strikers, so my reaction times and footwork improved – things I knew would help me with what was now a decade-long quest to play regularly for Australia. And when Tony Gustavsson took over the Matildas in September 2020, it felt like a fresh start.

12.

Tokyo Tears

Because goalkeepers operate so separately from the rest of the squad, I haven't really had a close relationship with most national team head coaches. Staj is an obvious exception, probably because I knew him for such a long time – I had a closeness with him that I haven't felt with anyone since. The downside is that the coach makes the final call on who starts any given match. The goalkeeper coach has a big say but ultimately doesn't have the power. When Tony G. was appointed, none of us really knew him. To a certain extent, we still only partially know him. He has told me he deliberately keeps a personal distance from his players so he can make impartial selection decisions based on form only. That makes sense but even if I'd known that back in the early days of his tenure, I don't think it would have made a difference. My head was all over the place, controlled by a constant hum of unwanted thoughts. I had a special capacity to ruminate on small interactions with coaches, internally magnifying them to the point that they took on a meaning that may or may not have existed. My mind jumped to conclusions, over-generalised and cata-strophised. Minimised the positive and homed in on the negative.

This affected me a lot and was exacerbated by my position in the pecking order. Tony G. had three levels of contact with his players. He interacted the most with Sam and Steph, his captain and vice-captain. The next rung down was his regular starting XI, who he trusted and rarely changed, unless he had to. And then there was the rest of the squad, with whom he had minimal direct com-munication. I was in the latter camp, which only fuelled my negative self-talk. When I arrived in camp there was usually a quick 'hello', followed several days later by a 'goodbye'.

My first experiences of this were during Tony's first international windows in charge, during the first half of 2021. I had been sidelined for two months with an MCL tear and was just on the verge of returning for my club in April when the Matildas were due to play two friendlies, against Germany and the Netherlands. I wasn't supposed to be available for these, as I still hadn't returned to playing and there was still a risk I could have reinjured my knee; and West Ham staff were reluctant to release me. But I was training fully and wanted so badly to make an impression. Fellow goalkeeper Teagan Micah was also unavailable, so I had a feeling it was an opportunity. In the end, West Ham let me go. They have always been so supportive of my ambitions with the national team. They knew all about my struggles and did whatever they could to help me.

The early days, aged seven, playing for Burleigh Bulldogs, and with my cat, Tiger, who Mum and Dad got me for my eighth birthday.

I always looked up to my brother and, like all younger siblings, followed him everywhere. This is us before a family wedding, and a school photo while we were both attending Marymount College.

The Palm Beach Currumbin State High School soccer team. Our teacher and coach, the late Kate Gleeson, lost a bet with us and had to wear a full-body swimsuit on this game day.

I was obsessed with the Brisbane Broncos from an early age and would kit up to watch them play. Meeting the boys after the 2023 World Cup was something eight-year-old me could never have imagined.

In action during my W-League debut for Perth Glory in 2011. *(Marne de Klerk/Getty Images)*

After stints with Canberra and Western Sydney, I was glad Jamie Harnwell accepted me back at the Glory in 2014 – we won that year's Premier's Plate and I was named goalkeeper of the year. History repeated itself on both counts with Brisbane Roar in 2017–18.

TOP: Hanging out with Sam and Teigen Allen during an early Matildas camp on the Gold Coast.

BOTTOM: Happy about my return to the national team set-up at the 2015 Cyprus Cup.

(Ann Odong)

Tournament fever with the girls at the Tokyo Olympics. *(Ann Odong/Australian Olympic Committee)*

ABOVE: Signing for West Ham in 2020 – one of the best decisions I ever made.
RIGHT: My first pre-season at Chadwell Heath. *(West Ham United FC)*

My first Christmas with Kirsty, soaking up the festivities under lights in London.

Girls on tour: Sam and me in London, hanging with Cait in Sydney, at a camp in Turkey, travelling in Asia, between training sessions in Florida and a lift selfie during our camp on the Gold Coast before the 2023 World Cup.

With Lydia and Teagan. Being a goalkeeper is a unique position, both competing with and learning from your teammates. *(Maddie Meyer/FIFA/Getty Images)*

The two Tonys: with Tony Gustavsson after our pre–World Cup friendly win against China, and taking instruction from Tony Franken ahead of the second half of our group game against Nigeria. *(Andy Cheung/Getty Images; Rachel Bach/By The White Line)*

The moment I saved a penalty during our World Cup quarter-final shootout with France . . .
(Bradley Kanaris/Getty Images)

. . . and the reaction of the girls. *(Justin Setterfield/Getty Images)*

My first major press conference appearance, in front of the international press on the day before our semi-final against England. *(Rachel Bach/By The White Line)*

ABOVE: Before Nike started selling goalkeeper jerseys, these Matildas fans made their own. *(The Croissants/@croissants_on_tour)*
RIGHT: Cait, Alanna and me, taking over the hotel hallway with our sticker books.

With friends and family
after the England game.

With Cait after the third-place playoff against Sweden. *(Rachel Bach/By The White Line)*

Through all the highs and lows, the support of my loved ones has meant everything to me.

I'm so proud of what the Matildas have accomplished, and what it will mean for the next generation of footballers in this country. But I'm not done yet. *(Xinhua News Agency/Getty Images)*

That camp didn't start well at all. We had to travel a bit to get to Wiesbaden, not far from Frankfurt. I recall a flight and then a bus ride. I got a phone call from Mum as I was getting off the bus. She was ringing to let me know my nana had died – her mum this time, the one who lived in Wollongong. The scene is still so clear to me. Alanna, Caitlin and I were doing our usual thing and stuffing around, and when I picked up the phone Caitlin was being a dickhead and yelling, 'Get off the phone' – just silly stuff we always did to each other. But Alanna was reading my face and could tell something was off. She grabbed Caitlin and told her to stop. Something about the unusual tone of Mum's voice tipped me off before she even told me. I was in tears as soon as she broke the news. The feeling was two-fold: I had just lost another grandparent, and this was another time that my family was going through something and I couldn't be there for them. My mum had just lost her mum and I couldn't give her a hug. It was actually quite sad for Caitlin, too. She lived down the road from Nana in Wollongong and had spent some time with her while I was visiting, enjoying those cups of tea and biscuits.

CAITLIN FOORD

I was super upset when Macca told me her nan had passed, because I had seen the bond they had and I knew her as well. Macca was just so upset. All we could do was be there for her. I went through my photos and found pictures and videos that I had taken with her nana and sent them to her. I figured they were nice memories to have.

The Matildas staff asked if I wanted us to wear black arm-bands for the first game against Germany or the second one against the Netherlands. I asked if I would be play-ing in either and they couldn't really tell me. But I had a feeling I might be in contention for the second friendly so I chose that one. I had already, by that time, endured the baptism of fire that was my first Matildas training session since my injury. It went from zero to 100 in a few min-utes. Tony Franken's son Jordan was the goalkeeper coach for that camp. He smacked the ball hard and didn't let up. But I welcomed the intensity, in a way, because I wanted to show I was ready to play. Lyds played against Germany – a 5–2 loss – and then we travelled to the Dutch city of Nijmegen. I was named in the starting line-up and we all wore black armbands. Unfortunately, we lost that game 5–0 and I played like shit. I wanted to play well for my nana but with every goal that went in, I thought, 'I could have done better with that.' It was probably the first time that I consciously realised I probably shouldn't have played. I had rushed myself back to begin with and now I was grieving as well. I had missed another time to be there for my family and missed another chance to perform for the Matildas. Both were so important to me – and I didn't exe-cute on either front. I went back to West Ham in a terrible headspace.

Really, that was just the start of everything going to shit before the Olympics and I really screwed myself in the next international window. In June, we played Denmark in Horsens and I was given another start. I thought it might go well, too, because Steph and Ellie were back in the side, and Sam came very close to scoring after only four minutes. It did not work out the way I'd hoped. After 25 minutes, we were 3–0 down. In the fifth minute, Tameka, in an attempt to clear a free kick, chipped an own goal over my head. Six minutes later, Denmark doubled their lead from a set piece. The corner came in and pinged around the box for several seconds. The play was so messy and the ball came at me from the goalmouth again and again. When a header hit the post, I ended up on my knees and couldn't recover in time to even try to get to Rikke Sevecke's follow-up into the roof of the net.

That wasn't even the worst thing that happened that game. Four minutes after that, a cross flew in. It looked innocuous at first but as it got closer its flight path fell almost in line with my near post. I hesitated, unsure if I was going to crash into the post en route to gathering the ball. So I jumped in an attempt to cover the area in case it made contact. But it missed the post and hit my gloves. From there, I ended up pushing it back into the post, only for it to rebound into the net. I had scored an own goal and I knew it was a bad mistake. Even though Mary and Polks scored late to make the full-time scoreline a more respectable 3–2, I knew I had played like absolute trash.

In hindsight, I knew deep down that I had fucked up my chance to claim the no. 1 spot, so I don't know what delusional part of me believed Tony G. would give me another chance in the next friendly, against Sweden five days later. I guess I just hoped that, because Lyds was out of this camp injured and Teagan had not yet made her international debut, he might have looked favourably on my experience with the national team.

The closer the game got, the more I believed my own narrative. Teagan hadn't even been capped and I'd been here for almost 10 years, and for those two reasons combined, I would be given a chance to redeem myself. Well, it became obvious during training the day before the game that Tony was going to play Teagan. I deserved to be benched, even if I had adopted a victim mentality about it. On match-day morning, once it had been confirmed, I went down to breakfast. The hotel we were staying at was configured in such a way that meant you had to walk through reception to get from the lift to the restaurant. Once I had finished and was passing reception to head back up to my room, I saw Tony G. having a chat with Teagan. He was talking to her about the game and encouraging her to be confident. It was then that I understood she was about to make her debut.

Later that day, I watched from the bench as we drew 0–0 with Sweden and Teagan was named player of the match. Even then, I tried to convince myself I had a shot of making the Olympics, even though I knew Tony would only take two goalkeepers as part of an 18-player squad, and Lyds was the first choice at the time. I was playing well for West Ham, so that had to count for something, surely.

It did not. The squad was to be selected a fortnight later and this had been the last camp to prove ourselves. I had played one not-so-great game and one terrible game, and Teagan had played one excellent game – and that was enough to knock me out. I can see now that Tony G. didn't owe me anything – he didn't owe anyone anything. At the time, though, I thought he was a prick who didn't cut me any slack. I was ready to quit.

When a major tournament is approaching, an extended squad is called into pre-camp and the selections are announced in person, after a period of time training together. Before the Tokyo Games, this pre-camp took place in Sweden. I chucked everything at it and trained really well. So well, in fact, that I thought I might be okay. After our last training session, each player was given a time slot for an individual meeting with the coaching staff, during which they would inform us of whether or not we had made the cut. It felt a bit like how I imagine a mass round of redundancies would go down in a workplace. We were all comparing notes in an attempt to glean some clues about what our specified time meant. Mine was very early in the afternoon, while Alanna's and Caitlin's were both very late. Caitlin Cooper's was a little earlier than mine and she was stressed because she was either going to be taken as an emergency player or not at all. We both started to put two and two together. By the time it was my turn, I knew what I was walking into.

In the room were Tony G., goalkeeper coach John Gorza and assistant coach Mel Andreatta. Tony gave me a slip of paper that had 'provisional player' written on it. He asked me if I had anything to say about what I had read. When I said that I did not, he then told me I had played my way out of the Olympic team, that Teagan had played her way in, and that Lydia had been selected as the second goalkeeper for her experience. Angry tears came. I declared I would not come as a provisional player and that it was best for me to go home. Tony offered me a day to think about it but I told him my decision was not going to change. I was just so angry at the whole situation and couldn't fathom even thinking of myself as nothing more than an injury replacement who travels with the team and trains but isn't an active part of it.

After the meeting, I avoided going back to the hotel, because I knew all the girls were there and it would prompt questions. So I went to sit down by the water and called my dad to tell him I'd been cut. I was so upset. He kept asking me if I was okay. I said over and over that I wanted to come home. I think he was a bit shocked by that, because I had never expressed a desire to leave the Matildas before – and I'm sure a part of him wanted me not to quit. But he told me that if I wanted to come home then I should come home, and he and Mum would support me. Once we were off the phone, I messaged Alanna. By the time she had called me and come to find me, I was sitting with Caitlin C. and Amy Harrison, who had both also been cut. Lans asked what I was going to do. 'I want to go home,' I said. 'I just can't be here right now.' Her response just made me cry more. 'No, Mac,' she said. 'Please come. I really need you.' Then she started tearing up, too, and said I didn't understand how much of an impact I have on the team. 'I know it's shit that you're not in but we really need you off the field as well.' Even then, I told her there was no fucking way I was staying.

ALANNA KENNEDY

That was probably the most hurt I've seen her, in that kind of situation. The first thing I said to her was, 'You can't leave. I know this is going to be really, really hard for you. It's a non-negotiable that you can't go home.' Selfishly, I wanted her there, but I also knew it was the right decision for her and for her future as a Matilda to stay and show the coaches and everyone who doubted her. Because, at the end of the day, I don't think it came down to her ability. She struggled with her confidence and mindset, and sometimes attitude with certain things. And so I felt like that was the best opportunity for her to turn that around.

Eventually, we returned to the hotel and saw everyone. They were all gutted and it was warming to see how affected they were by the decision. Sam came up to me and said she had told Tony he'd made a mistake and that I didn't deserve to be omitted. It felt like Sam and the whole team had my back and everyone just sat with me. In retrospect, I have a far more complete understanding about why I didn't make the team. Objectively speaking, I wasn't bringing my club form to the national team and the coach made a call he was entitled to make. But my mindset at the time was one of pure frustration and deep insecurity. I had waited, and waited, and waited, and then it was all taken away from me at the final hurdle. In my mind, I was 27 years old and still failing at the thing I had been working towards since I was a teenager.

Alanna asked me what I would do when I went home. I told her I was done with football. That I might play AFLW, if that was still an option. I would do literally anything except sit on the Matildas' bench for another 10 years.

It's pretty amazing what a few hours around good friends can do to shift your perspective. How motivating feeling needed can be. How time can calm you down. By the end of that evening, I had changed my mind and agreed to come and support them. I also realised that I probably shouldn't leave football, as I needed to earn a living and West Ham were paying me after all. The next day, after speaking with the girls and my family, I asked Tony and Mel for a meeting. It was very informal but I told them I was struggling to come to terms with their decision. Despite that, I said, I had decided to come as a provisional player. I also told them I wanted to make it clear that I was not doing this for them. I had to say that last bit. I needed them to know the only reason I would put myself through such an ostracising experience was to be there for the team. To be fair to Tony, he said he understood completely; that he also believed the girls needed me and he really appreciated my decision. I also expressed that I found it confusing that he and I had never had a conversation despite him now having been in the role for nine months. 'I want you to know that I've done that on purpose,' he replied. 'I've tried to keep my distance from everyone, so I don't form any attachment to anyone and can just purely base my decision off what I see.'

The very next day, as if by some cruel twist of fate, the International Olympic Committee changed the rules to allow each country an extra four players in their squads. The call was made to give teams some flexibility while the COVID-19 pandemic was still having its way with the health and logistics of sporting organisations and athletes. Our manager Gina delivered me the news in the meal room and all the girls ran over and gave me the biggest hugs. In reality, it didn't really change anything. But I was officially part of the Olympic squad and that felt nice. Then Tony came over with this big smile on his face and gave me a hug, too. I remember thinking, 'Ergh, this doesn't change a thing.' But have to admit I also appreciated the sentiment.

That rule change meant I was included in most Olympic-related activities, and I received the uniform and gear. Initially, I anticipated that these little extras would make for an overall good experience in Japan. In reality, the tournament was just as mentally challenging for me. On the one hand, because the pressure was off, I trained my arse off every single day. I trained probably the best I've trained in my whole career. Once each match day rolled around, though, the sense of rejection felt just as sharp as it had felt on selection day weeks prior. My quality of training meant nothing, because I felt I was just a spare part. Outside of a few difficult experiences, I rarely feel down for long periods of time. As a general rule, I prefer to smile and get on with life, even if I'm agonising over something internally. On this tour, I spent a lot more time alone in my room. After a couple of hours, I was usually able to bounce back enough to continue with the routine. I also had a lot of support from Steph Catley. She had a rough Olympics off the field and we confided in each other quite a bit and became pretty close.

These moments at rock bottom were speckled throughout fun times. The Olympic Village was exciting and full of interesting athletes from all around the world, and it is impossible to travel with the Matildas and not spend a good chunk of time laughing about something or other. But it did not offset the emptiness I felt during each of Australia's six matches that I watched from the stands. I did not make it onto the bench once all tournament. That meant that, had we won a medal instead of finishing fourth, I would not have received one. Almost every one of the other 11 nations competing in the women's football tournament made sure to swap players on the bench with all of those left in the stands at least once, to ensure every member of the squad was eligible for a medal. That wouldn't have been the case for me or Elise Kellond-Knight, and KK was injured and no chance of playing. It left me with conflicted feelings. Of course I wanted the Matildas to win a medal but I don't know how I would have been able to watch the entire squad be presented with one and be left out of it. There was and is guilt associated with this sentiment but I was also just trying to get through every day until I could get on a plane out of there.

We ended up losing our bronze-medal match to the United States and the girls were devastated. It is one thing to lose a semi-final and know you will not have a chance to compete for gold, but it cuts especially deep to be on the verge of medalling at a major tournament and leave with nothing physical to show for it. I was numb and also heightened at the same time; unable to let it all out but aware something small could open the floodgates.

In the end, it was the resignation of our physio, Dave Battersby. He announced this would be his last tour during dinner and drinks on the final night. Dave was much loved and his tears set off several others in the room, including me. I was actually quite close with him – on top of his Matildas duties, he was also a physio on the Gold Coast, so I regularly went to see him while I was at home. And he had been so good with me during this trip. The mixture of Dave's departure with everything else felt overwhelming – once I began to cry, I couldn't stop.

It didn't get any better after the speeches, either. Once everyone started mingling, lots of players and staff approached me to say how proud they were of me for getting through the tournament and the way I held myself under the circumstances. Every person who said something set me off again. I can't tell you how much I cried. There were so many emotions and I was so relieved it was over. I don't regret my decision to go to the Olympics. I believe it was the right thing to do and I would make the same decision again. But I also hope I never have to.

13.
Tony Franken

The Olympics also marked the last tour for another member of staff. It was after the end of our campaign that I ran into John Gorza in the hallway at our hotel. He stopped me to let me know he wouldn't be returning. I didn't know what to say. It was news to me but I also wasn't surprised. When Ante finished up in mid-2020, Lydia and I had a conversation about our current coaching situation. We both really like John as a person. He was lovely in every respect and did genuinely seem to want the best for us. We just didn't believe he had the capacity to get the best out of us on the field. That was probably partly because we were both long-time students of Jonesy, who was on our backs about everything and didn't allow mistakes. Healthy or not, it made us sharp. I went from that to a coach who was a nice guy who didn't really serve it that hard. If you made a mistake, it was okay. I felt like I plateaued and wasn't getting the best out of myself. So it was a bit awkward when John told me he was leaving but I thanked him and wished him all the best. Then I wondered who might replace him. When Lyds and I spoke about getting a new coach, we knew we wanted somebody with no previous connection to any of the goalkeepers. Basically, somebody completely neutral, whose opinion we could all trust without question.

I can't remember if Tony Franken's name was mentioned to me before he first lobbed into camp in September 2021. I hadn't met him at this point but of course knew the name. His status within the Socceroos over more than a decade is the stuff of legend. He's worked with Mark Schwarzer, Zeljko Kalac and Mat Ryan, and with head coaches Guus Hiddink, Ange Postecoglou and Graham Arnold across the 2006, 2010, 2014 and 2018 men's World Cups. Initially, Tony F. came to us just to help fill the gap post-Olympics after John left. He was busy as it was with his role as head of goalkeeping for FA, overseeing the development of goalkeeper coaches from the professional game right down to community football. But a couple of sessions in, Lyds, Teagan and I all knew he was the one for us.

> **TONY FRANKEN, goalkeeper coach**
>
> I was asked to come in just for the away friendly against Ireland. We had a team meeting with just the goalkeepers. The girls were fractionally late and I laid down the law and told them it wasn't acceptable. That's probably the first contact I had with Mackenzie. But I came in with a clean slate. Obviously, I knew Lydia had nearly 100 caps. Mackenzie was sort of the second in line but really didn't take her chances when she had an opportunity at international level, and then

you had Teagan. So I didn't have any so-called favourites or someone I thought was better than the others. If you're playing well, you'll play, and if you're not playing, you'll be told why. I've used that method all the way through and I think the girls respect that. One thing I noticed was that the women don't want to be treated any differently to the men. They tell me to kick it as hard as I normally would. So I tend to exercise what I call tough love but not in a brutal way. More in the sense that these are the standards and this is what I expect. And I think they appreciate that.

Tony was that neutral presence we all needed, which meant we were all completely comfortable accepting whatever decision he made in terms of selections. The added bonus was that he had seen and done everything and been around the block. He was all business, too. When we'd come out for training, he would offer a quick, 'How are you girls?' and then get straight into it – 'This is what we're doing.' The more we got to know him, the more we worked out his personality. He was definitely up for a joke here and there. On the whole, however, he is pretty serious and wants the job done properly. Tony isn't interested in messing around, which is similar to how Jonesy was. But he differed from Jonesy in that he wasn't interested in knowing our personal lives. When we came to training, he expected us to be switched on at all times, but what we did off the field belonged to us.

That last bit is interesting to me in hindsight, because there were times he seemed to know instinctively what I needed off the field, despite not being very involved in my personal life. It was like he could read my body language and tell when I was up and about and when I was struggling – even when I needed to be told off. He is emotionally intelligent and has coached enough players to develop a knack for it.

Because of the pandemic, I still hadn't been home since I signed for West Ham, and late October 2021 was going to mark my return. We had a two-match friendly series against Brazil scheduled in Sydney. It's safe to say I did not imagine I would contract my first dose of COVID four days after landing in Australia and right before our first game. We were all testing regularly and I was definitely not feeling well. Our head of performance at the time, Paddy Steinfort, pulled me aside and told me the news straight after our match-day-minus-one training session at Parramatta's CommBank Stadium. I know this is becoming a theme, but yes, I started crying. I knew I'd have to go into isolation and the personal recounts weren't very positive. At first, I was moved to an apartment suite in the same hotel but on a higher floor from the rest of the girls. That meant they could still bring me coffees and snacks and whatever else I needed. After a couple of days, however, the rules dictated that I had to move to a government-run COVID hotel. Matildas staff did everything they could to keep me in the same building but it was essentially out of their hands.

That was probably the saddest thing, because I had to wait until everyone had left for the game, then pack my stuff and take it all downstairs where a sealed-up transfer van was waiting for me. I was given a hazmat suit and mask to wear, to protect the driver. It felt very dramatic and I was scared. That soon changed, as I was fortunate enough to be provided a fully equipped apartment with a kitchen and balcony. Breakfast of fruit, cereal and juice was delivered in a paper bag at the start of the day and frozen meals came for lunch and dinner, courtesy of the government. FA looked after me by giving me an allowance for Uber Eats and anything else I needed. They also had a treadmill and some other exercise equipment delivered to keep me busy, which was a lifesaver. One of my old friends who lived in Sydney also brought me over his PlayStation and a collection of games, which saw me through the lonelier hours. Bless him. I spent 10 days in iso. Once I tested negative, I was driven straight to Sydney airport to fly back to London. So much for the trip home. I finally made it for real a month later, when we played a two-match series against the US. It was worth the wait.

14.
Meet Cute

It was the British summer of 2022 and I was not looking for a relationship. And when I say this, I mean I was pretty committed to staying single for at least a year or two. It had only been five months since my ex and I had broken up, after four years together. We had done the majority of it long distance, which took a lot out of me, and I needed time to just be with myself for a bit. Of course, it's little surprise that I met someone immediately and was completely taken with her. Kirsty Smith was just a name among a list of names announced as off-season signings. Jess Ziu. Halle Houssein. Kirsty Smith. A Scottish full-back coming from Manchester United. That was the start and end of my knowledge. I knew nothing else about her. But the minute I saw her on the first day of pre-season, I knew I was in trouble. I was making myself some toast in our old meal room and she was standing a few metres away. I went over and said, 'Hey, I'm Mac. Nice to meet you,' and gave her a hug like I would to any new player. Then I went back to making my toast.

I knew right away I was very attracted to her but tried to ignore it for the first couple of weeks. We had these little interactions during training – I don't know if you would call it flirting but it was definitely banter. If she missed a goal or I saved it, I'd take the piss a bit and we'd have a laugh. About three weeks in, once we had started conversing more regularly around training, at meals or in the gym, I realised I was probably paying more attention to her than I thought. It felt like the feeling might be mutual but couldn't be sure, so I played it cool for a bit. Within no time, though, I'd had enough of this and DM'd her on Instagram after training one day. 'Coffee?' I wrote. Then I waited. An hour passed before she saw it and by that time it was 4 p.m. and she had just arrived home. I was at home at that point, too, and we agreed it was too late but that we would another day. That opened the line of communication and we started chatting. A couple of days after that, we went out for brunch and from then we were inseparable. The only issue was that we didn't want anybody else at West Ham to know yet – we wanted to feel our way through on our own while it was still relatively new. That was problematic because I was flatting with another girl in our team and Kirsty was still in a house with three other players while she was looking for her own place. We couldn't hang out at either of our homes without somebody finding out.

The only real way we could get to know each other in private was to go for walks together. For the entire next month, we walked almost every afternoon. All around London. For hours. Under normal circumstances, we would both be over it within 20 minutes. We covered so much of the city on foot, taking different routes each day.

Every other day, we went to the park and sat there for hours just talking. Then walk a lap and sit down again. We actually had to find a new park early on, which was a little inconvenient but necessary – some of our teammates started going to the one we initially picked and we couldn't risk them bumping into us together. So we found a new green space to chill until dinner time. Even then, we didn't want to leave. Sometimes, we walked to Nando's and grabbed something to eat before heading to our respective homes to sleep, then woke up for training in the morning and did it all again. Eventually, Kirsty found an apartment, which meant I could have dinner and hang out at hers.

The whole thing was just crazy and so unplanned. But we took it very slowly. Part of the reason was that it took me a while to convince Kirst I wasn't going to break her heart. It was a challenge and it took a while. She had been through a tough experience in the past, so was understandably hesitant. But I obviously knew by this point that she had feelings for me, so we went at a comfortable pace for both of us. I had jumped into past relationships quite quickly, so this felt unusual and at times I second-guessed what was happening. In the end, however, it felt right. We were doing it properly and building the foundations of something pretty special.

As soon as Kirsty moved into her flat, I was over there all the time. And as it became more obvious to everyone that we were together, I moved in. Her place was closer to our training ground, she was on her own and my room-mate was due to move to Liverpool at the end of the season. It made financial sense, too, given I was paying rent for a home I was hardly at and that money could help Kirsty share the cost of her rent. We took the view that if it didn't work out, we'd deal with it. Thankfully, we haven't needed to. Our living and training arrangements mean we spend almost every waking moment together.

We're opposites in a lot of ways. I'm quite outgoing, she is quieter. I'm more rash with decisions, she takes time to think about things. I'm stubborn, she's understanding. So she balances me out and helps me see the other side to a lot of situations (that in itself can trigger my stubborn-ness but I come around eventually). In this sense, we've helped each other with our mindsets. Especially as team captain, I could be quite direct in my approach and Kirsty helped me add a little empathy into the mix.

KIRSTY SMITH, partner

I didn't really know of Mac before I met her. When I arrived at West Ham, I didn't approach her – or anyone else, really – because I'm such a quiet person. But she was one of the first people to come over and speak to me and introduce herself. She gave me a hug and just made it so comfortable. I thought it was really nice she made the effort, especially as I didn't know many people.

I knew I was coming into an already-established team, where everyone already had their friend groups and relationships. It was the first time I'd ever had to deal with that situation – I had joined

Manchester United in its foundation season and we were all new then and in the same boat. And I think sometimes people can almost get a wrong impression of me – I am not someone who finds it easy to just approach someone I don't know and chat away, so there's a risk people think I don't want to talk to them. But Mackenzie made the effort and decided she would get to know me. It took me a few months to feel comfortable at the club but Mackenzie invited me out with her friends and made me feel welcome, and then the pair of us started to talk and spend a lot more time together.

Early on, when I was struggling a bit, it was affecting me on the training pitch – it almost got too much for me. She was always just there, making sure I was okay. Not with grand gestures or anything; just by saying little things that would make me laugh. There was a time early on when I fell ill and felt so shitty I ended up leaving training to go home. Mackenzie came around to my place with a little care package. She had bought me some tablets, some chocolate and a drink. At that point, I could see she really cared. Still, I wanted to be really cautious with it for the first few months, just to make sure it was right. It was pretty obvious to both of us that we liked each other but I wanted to take it slow at the beginning to avoid getting hurt or into a sticky situation that affected the team if it didn't work out. We also spoke a lot about what that player had said; she kept assuring me that wasn't who she is. I think that was difficult for her to overcome – that from the beginning, when she hadn't actually done anything wrong, someone had planted a seed in my head. I should have cut her a bit more slack.

It's mad how many hours we spent walking. Who knew a walk could be so fun? If we went for a walk now, we would genuinely hate it. But we just wanted to be in each other's company and the time passed so quickly. It was actually good we met in summer because we could sit outside and not have to feel freezing cold.

I don't know how true this is but people have made little comments about the change in Mac since we've been together. That she's more calm. I do know that we work well together. I calm her down and she brings me out of my shell. I'm also quite a focused and driven person and I think a little bit of that might have brushed off onto her free spirit. We bring out good things in each other's personalities that maybe weren't there before.

15.
Turning Point

I played a total of two Matildas matches in 2022. Technically, it was actually one and a half. The first was our opener at the 2022 Asian Cup, held in India in January and February. That game, an 18–0 win over Indonesia, was the high point for everyone, to be honest. We did win all our group games but were knocked out in the quarters by South Korea. Not much about that tournament felt overly good. We had high hopes of winning it and it went to shit. Our performances aside, COVID was still running rampant in India. Meeks tested positive and took her turn to be escorted out in a hazmat suit. We couldn't really leave the hotel in Mumbai unless we were training or playing. After our premature exit, headlines started flying around that Tony G. should get the sack. But as long as he was manager, Tony was the person I needed to prove myself to. Every time I went into camp, I knew I had to be on. I couldn't afford to take my foot off the pedal because I had a point to prove.

My second and final appearance of 2022 was an unmitigated disaster. In June, we travelled to Huelva to play world no. 7 Spain. Teagan started, which I assumed meant she was playing the full 90. Aitana Bonmatí, who was clearly already well on the way to winning the 2023 Ballon d'Or, put her side ahead with a wonderful strike to give Spain a 1–0 lead going into the break. Usually, when the half-time whistle blows, we all head straight into the changerooms. But Tony F. asked me to warm up with him instead. I said, 'Wait, what? Am I going on?' He replied in the affirmative. My immediate thought was: 'Any fucking chance they could have let me know in advance?' It's just so hard to sit on the bench and then have this sprung on you. And it so rarely happens with goalkeepers. They were obviously testing whether I was in the right mindset and ready to go. On the outside, I was, in the sense that I warmed up and ran on for the start of the second half. On the inside, I was so far from ready. 'We're about to get battered,' I thought. 'I hope I don't make a mistake.' If I was going to get a chance, I wanted it to be a proper one, not just be thrown to the wolves as part of a second-string line-up.

For this window, Tony G. had given his star players a break in a bid to avoid burnout a year out from the 2023 World Cup. It meant Sam, Cait, Lans, Hayley and the like weren't selected for this trip. So we were a less-experienced team against a full-strength Spain, just trying to stay in it. We did not stay in it. By the 57th minute, the score was 4–0; by full-time, it was 7–0. The highlights package is basically just of me conceding goal after goal. I had blown my chance to play at a home World Cup. I was fuming. It was central to my mindset at the time – to play the 'unfair' card. And this was the epitome of unfairness. I don't like that I was always making excuses as to why I didn't play well or get another chance, but I sought out Tony afterwards and basically told him the whole situation was fucking bullshit and that we were always going to get pumped. He told me I needed to control what I could control but all I could think about was what had happened just before the Tokyo Olympics, and also what had happened after. I had returned to West Ham so focused on my club football. The national team had not been a happy space for me at that time but at West Ham I felt valued and played consistently well. So I had spent the good part of 12 months building myself back up in London, only to have another terrible national team experience that set me back mentally once again. I was just so frustrated.

Part of what Tony F. was trying to tell me about controlling the controllables was that I needed to take charge of my own headspace regardless of the environment around me. I felt so good at West Ham because the structure around me was so supportive. I had to learn how to transfer that internal energy over to the Matildas, even when I wasn't feeling the same level of support. I was two completely different players: one confident and comfortable, the other tentative and timid. When I did something well during Matildas training, Tony used to say, 'This is West Ham Macca.'

TONY FRANKEN

In the early days with Mackenzie, there was often an excuse or a reason why performances were the way they were. I told her I wasn't really interested in reasons and excuses, that I was only looking at performances. I would also say she wasn't as focused when I first came in. She was happy to do what she had to do at training without actually pushing. I'm not sure if that was psychological, if perhaps she had felt undervalued in the past. Over the years, she was always seen as a no. 2 and I don't think she felt that anyone at national team level believed in her. But it was obvious when she got an opportunity against Spain. Yes, we probably had a second XI out there but there were things in that match she could have done better. Sometimes you tell players they're coming on and sometimes you don't. Teagan was always going to play the first half but we weren't going to tell Macca she was coming on in the second because sometimes that happens in games – sometimes people get injured and you have to be ready. I don't like that being used as an excuse. She did send me a bit of a shitty text later and it was a bit 'woe is me'. I spoke to her afterwards and validated some of her concerns, but also asked her, 'At the end of the day, would you say you took your opportunity with both hands?' She said, 'Probably not.' And I said, 'Well, that's what we need to talk about.' So we talked about the performance rather than the other external factors, as a means of understanding the importance of blocking out external factors and worrying about what she is actually going to do. The turning point for me probably came in October 2022, while we were in Europe to play friendlies against South Africa and Denmark. The technical staff chose Teagan to play those two games and I could see Macca was very disappointed.

I was having a really good season with West Ham and doing everything right off the field. I still hadn't played for the Matildas since before the Olympics but had a good feeling in camp that this might be my time. My role in training hinted that they might start me at least once and I figured it would be the South Africa game, because they were ranked world no. 54 at the time and perceived as a reasonably easy opponent. Plus I lived in London and the game was being played in London. But then the selection meeting came and Teagan was once again named in goal. I was shattered. She was playing in Sweden at the time and her season had already finished. I was in the thick of mine and match fit. We went straight from the meeting to dinner and I hid my emotions as best as I could. Whenever I started to feel them creeping back in, I made an extra effort to joke with the girls. I felt confident that, to the outside observer, it appeared as if I didn't have a care in the world.

After dinner, as I was about to leave the meal room to head back to my room, Tony F. asked if I could meet him downstairs in a couple of minutes. When I arrived, we sat down and he asked whether I was okay. The question came as such a shock that I didn't have enough time to adopt the poker face I assumed had been so convincing. I replied that I wasn't really okay. I was already crying when I said it. I told Tony that I felt as if there was nothing else I could possibly do to get another chance. I was giving it everything I had and that still wasn't enough. I think part of the reason I felt so disheartened was that I had significantly changed my mindset over the preceding few months.

Tony just listened. It was kind of a moment he gave me to have a quick vent and let out everything I had been holding onto for so long. Then he said he understood and told me he believed I was doing all the right things. I think he might have expected me to play, too. He said I just had to keep doing everything I was doing so that, when my chance came, I would be ready to take it. He still didn't sugarcoat it. He didn't tell me I should be playing or even that I deserved to be playing, just kept reiterating that my time would come and that I had to be ready when it did. What I like is that he didn't simply tell me what I wanted to hear. But the way he showed he cared about me lit a fire inside me. I 1000 per cent wanted to play for Tony F. and this was enough to keep me going until I could.

BRUCE KAIDER, agent

My connection with Mac came through Alanna Kennedy. I've been representing Alanna for a number of years, and in 2020 or thereabouts she told me Mac was looking for a new agent. The pair of them are obviously pretty close, so when Alanna asked me if I would be interested in having a chat with Mac, I agreed. At that point, she hadn't really broken through. She had obvious, enormous potential — everyone knew what she was capable of. The question mark for me was around whether she was prepared or willing to put in the work required to be the very best at her craft.

A lot of the work we did early on was to help me understand her a bit more, to get to the bottom of where she was as an athlete and a person. We had a number of really difficult conversations and I think she was probably frustrated with me at various times. But, essentially, I told her that I have been fortunate to work with some of the very best athletes to come out of this country. People such as Matthew Dellavedova, Stephanie Rice, Lauren Jackson and Lydia Lassila. I told her that these athletes all have certain qualities and apply themselves in certain ways, and that I wasn't convinced that she had been applying herself in a similar way. And that, being completely honest, I don't necessarily like to work with people who aren't trying their best. I'm invested in my athletes but it has to be a 50/50 relationship. I'm prepared to give them 50 per cent but they have to give me their full 50 per cent, too. If they're only prepared to give me 30 per cent, I'll give them 30 per cent as well. But we're probably not going to do very well because together we're going to miss out on 40 per cent of the things we want. I told Mac we might not be a good fit moving forward. She wasn't all that happy to hear that. In her heart of hearts, she probably thought I was being a bit of an arsehole.

She definitely, at times, had a tendency to fall back on excuses. To complain that she wasn't supported or given something she needed. To me, excuses are irrelevant. You've got to control what you can control, and what you can control is your application to your craft. And from what I was hearing, she was happy to do enough, the bare minimum, but no more than she needed, and that probably explained why she was at where she was at with her career. 'You're good — you're not great,' I said. 'And you've got to decide whether you want to be that player or not.'

The thing was, I knew she was best friends with Alanna and Alanna is one of the hardest-working athletes I've been around in terms of her application and discipline. It stands to reason that Alanna sees something she loves in Mac as a person and as an athlete. And if that was true, perhaps she just needed the right people around her, those willing to support her but also challenge her in uncomfortable ways. I don't think she had enough people around her who were asking her questions and showing genuine care and interest in how her career was being shaped.

I ended up building a relationship with the West Ham women's team general manager, Aidan Boxall, during negotiations for her contract extension in mid-2022. I said to Aidan, 'Be honest with me, mate. Where do you see her?' He told me he believed she could be one of the best goalkeepers in the world, if not the best in the world, but she didn't do the work. That she was always last in and first out. She didn't cut corners or miss training sessions — she wasn't that person. But if training started at 8 a.m., she'd be there at 8 a.m. And if it finished at 4 p.m., she'd leave at 4 p.m. She didn't do any of the extra stuff like getting treatment or doing extra weights training. She basically did what she had to do to be a good player but none of the stuff that all the best players do in addition to that. I told Aidan I had now heard this consistently from a few people, including some of her teammates. I suggested we have a conversation with Mac together, for all of our benefit. We needed to get on the same page, because the contract she said she wanted was only going to come if she put in the effort.

This meeting ended up being a pivotal moment. We were both really blunt with her and gave her some home truths based on some of the things we had seen and heard. And the language got colourful. I told her I don't want to work with people who don't want to be the best they can be. It's just not who I am and it's not what I've committed my life to doing as an agent. I've got other people I could invest time and energy in, rather than wasting time with people who are really not interested. 'So fucking tell me,' I said. 'Are you committed? Do you want to actually do the work?'

Aidan is pretty colourful and pretty blunt, too. There are people who don't like him for those reasons but I love him. He was one of Mackenzie's key supporters, to the point that the contract extension he offered her came with far more money than she deserved at the time. Mac wasn't even close to the player who'd usually receive that kind of contract. That was his handshake commitment to her up front. He basically advance paid her, put his balls on the block as a way of telling her he was in – and now she had to show she was in, too. I love that he did that and I have so much respect for him for it. Because she could have been a flop. Had Mac continued in the same manner as before and remained the same level of athlete, then he would have well and truly overpaid for what she was delivering. But given she went and did what she has done, she's bloody cheap.

At first, her face showed no emotion. She just listened and looked down the barrel. Then I think she was embarrassed. And then I could see she was pissed off with both of us. We were arseholes. Fair enough – we were being pretty stern with her. But she took the feedback on quietly; I don't know many athletes who would eat the humble pie in the way that she did during that meeting. It's all very well for us to reflect on it now and say we were the catalyst for all this change but that conversation could easily have gone the other way. Mac could have cracked it afterwards, sacked me, told Aidan to get fucked and left West Ham. I think, though, in her heart of hearts, she knew some of this was true. And she was being told it by two people she knew genuinely believed in her and wanted her to be better; who were investing time and energy and contract support to help her reach the next level. She just had to do the work. And to her credit, she fuckin' did it.

She went from being one of the back end of the group, in terms of physical testing, to one of the top three. Once she started to become a great athlete, she started playing better. Then she started changing her diet and sleeping better as well. And all of a sudden, things started to turn. I couldn't be happier for Mac. She didn't do it easy in her career up until the World Cup. And she's a great human being. Loyal, thoughtful, caring. Even after the team success of the World Cup, she has remained humble. I couldn't be more proud of what she's achieved.

That conversation was sort of brutal but it needed to happen. When I first joined West Ham, I was just having a really good time. I was living in London and meeting new teammates. I was playing relatively well but I can see now that there was so much of my approach that could have been better. That included gym, recovery and nutrition. I've never really loved the gym. I just find it boring. BK and Aidan basically just gave it to me – told me I needed to be a better all-round athlete. I didn't really expect that, in part because I wasn't playing badly. I was definitely more defensive at the start than I should have been but after a while we got on the same page and I understood where they were coming from. They just wanted the best for me and knew what I was capable of.

AIDAN BOXALL, women's team general manager, West Ham

Me and BK got right into her, to be fair: 'I know you can be the best goalkeeper in the world. There's no two ways about it. The question is: A – do you believe it? And B – what are you going to do about it? Because you keep dicking about and I can understand why you're not getting picked for the Matildas. If you are going into camp acting and behaving like you are, you ain't going to get selected. It's not going to happen. It's not going to happen. So you can moan and bitch about it, or you can do what you need to do.

'Mate, listen – you need to understand something. Potentially, you are going to have a home World Cup, which will include a group game in your home city. How many players on this planet can say they've played a home World Cup game in their home city in front of all their friends and family? If you don't pull your fucking finger out, you won't be able to look at yourself in the mirror for the rest of your days, because you'll know you didn't do everything you could to make that happen. If you pull your finger out, you will be no. 1 – no question about it.'

We went back and forth like this for a bit and I think the penny started to drop. So I put the money on the table and basically said, 'Don't make me look an idiot. I believe in you.' I've always believed in her. The manager at the time wanted her gone – and I can understand why – but I put my neck on the line to defend her. But at the same time, it was a case of, 'Now you've got what you want and you need to deliver. No bullshit. And that means you need to be playing that World Cup.'

I have so much respect for the way she handled that conversation. Only the three of us knew it had happened. And she knows I've always fought in her corner. I've had conversations with players in similar situations and they've always blamed everyone else – coaches, staff, the club – and not looked to themselves. But Macca had the balls to actually look at herself and go, 'No, you're right. I need to sort it out.' She took it on the chin and she squared up, and the rest is history.

It's funny – after we had that conversation, we played Man City and I saw Alanna. She goes, 'What the fuck have you done with her? That ain't the same kid. She's come back to camp and she has her head down.' After she started working, guess who's our best overall athlete? Power, strength, everything. Even I was laughing.

But still she was going to camp and not being picked. When she came home after being beaten 7–0 by Spain, she was so devastated I had to scrape her off the floor. She took that really personally and became snappy and withdrawn. That's when I said, 'Enough's enough. That ain't on.' I went after Football Australia then, because I was concerned about her welfare. She'd be in a great place when she left here for camp and then come back a totally different person. Sometimes, in the earlier days, I'd ask her if she'd done everything she could possibly do. And she'd be like, 'Yeah. Well, um, maybe no.' And I said, 'Well, what are you expecting then?' However, I had seen her change in attitude with my own eyes – she was up there with the best goalkeepers in the world. I emailed FA's performance director, Paddy Steinfort, and the Matildas' team manager, Gina Rees, to ask for a meeting with Tony Gustavsson to understand why she wasn't being given feedback about what she needed to do to play. I never got one and honestly felt like pulling her out of the squad completely – just not releasing her, because it was killing her and we were having to rebuild her every time.

I felt for Tony Franken, to be fair. I first met him around that time and it was actually hilarious. He came over and spent a couple of days with us, sat with me to watch us play Brighton. So I was sitting there with Tony pre-game just having a laugh, and I asked him, 'Tony, what is going on here, mate? Why is she not playing for the national team?' He was trying to be diplomatic but I wouldn't let it go. 'She's the best goalkeeper in this league,' and this and that. Anyway, by the end of the game, Mac had smashed the ball, it'd hit a teammate and dropped into the path of the opposing forward, who rolled it into an empty net. She had an absolute stinker and I felt like I had given her the kiss of death. But bless him, Tony – the complete gentleman – he didn't say a bad word about Tony Gustavsson and was also very complimentary about Macca.

A good goalkeeper is as good as a top striker, because it's on her to make the difference. And more times than not, she has made the difference. A prime example would be our first win away at Manchester City. If it wasn't for her, we never would have left there with a clean sheet and three points. I'm a believer in karma. She took that conversation on the chin, had not only one but two opportunities to play in her home town in front of her friends and family, and she was the star of the show against France. Sitting there, watching that game, I couldn't have been prouder of her. She showed the world that night what she's about.

ALANNA KENNEDY

I can imagine Mac getting off that call with BK and Aidan and being like, 'Those fucking pricks.' But she knew that underneath the harsh words there was a foundation of friendship. And they could see what she could do. She was coming up against a lot of shots from very good WSL players and she was thriving. She's a fucking brilliant keeper.

A lot of athletes need good people around them. Even though footballers have teammates to talk to, it's still really important to have a circle of trust, those willing to tell you the truth. When it comes to elite athletes and high-profile people, many are scared to give them real feedback. People can tend to dance around the truth. I don't feel like that does anyone any favours. I'd prefer to give my honest opinion and feedback – with compassion and kindness, but always with the intention of getting the best out of people. Particularly people I care about a lot.

16.
Belonging

I don't want to say I accepted my position in the Matildas, but at some point in the second half of 2022 I began to view my selection – or non-selection – as uncontrollable. I realised all I could do was train and play the best that I could – if I got a chance, I got a chance. I stopped putting expectations on it. It's a difficult one to explain. Put it this way: I was shocked to get that first Cup of Nations game against Czechia in February 2023 and it was almost funny to me that I played well. The lack of expectation removed the internal pressure and that felt freeing on the field. The confidence wasn't even conscious.

Alanna and Caitlin used to try to build up my confidence all the time. Alanna would tell me I deserved to be no. 1 and that I shouldn't accept where I was in the pecking order. They definitely helped put things into perspective but something still had to change in me to accept their optimism in a way that was transferable into my game. I had always thought they said nice things about me because they were my friends. If I received the same from coaches, they were only saying it because they were my coaches. My default setting was to believe every compliment or word of encouragement was an act of pity, not authentic praise. It's just the kind of person I am, and it's something I've been consistently working on.

I wouldn't even say I became confident. I guess I just started to feel like I was enough, whether I was playing for Australia or not. Even now, I sit in a comfortable middle ground where I know I am a better goalkeeper than I believed I was for all those years but I also know I still have much further to go. I will never assume my position is safe but being able to walk into goal without having already undergone a pre-match session of self-flagellation was refreshing.

LYDIA WILLIAMS

I think the Olympics hurt her deep. You have to sit on your arse for a long time as a goalkeeper and wait for your opportunity. So I think when she was initially left out of the squad, she was like, 'No, I've done my time and a half. I've sat on the bench all this time and I'm not allowing this.' It clicked in her head that it takes a different mentality but she also started wanting to be among the action. Goalkeeping requires a lot of resilience and hers was built through missing out. Now there's maturity and expectation. She sees Mary Earps and others winning the WSL's golden glove and realises she plays against them at club level – that she can do what Earps does.

ALANNA KENNEDY

She's more talkative on the field now. There's more confidence in her communication and instruction, especially on set plays, when the keeper is key to organising the structure of the team. She's just a bit more professional, to be honest.

KIRSTY SMITH

When I first met Mac, we were both in and out of the national team. It's difficult and if you don't have that confidence, it's always going to affect you. So we kind of understood each other in that sense. Seeing her overcoming that part of it inspires me. Not many people can come out and just be like, 'Do you know what? I'm going to do this and it's going to work for me.' I am really proud of her for that.

One person who helped me in a big way without even realising it was Mark Schwarzer.

SAM ARNOLD

I reached out to Mark in the knowledge that he lived in the UK and gave him some context around what Kenz was going through. It was during her form slump and I put it down to confidence. I asked if he might have time to reach out to her.

Mark Schwarzer contacted me during that period around the Olympics. He offered advice and I offloaded a little bit of frustration. When he first made contact, I was pretty embarrassed that my big brother had reached out to him and I didn't want to hassle him. I just couldn't believe Mark had messaged me. What he said definitely resonated with me but it was more who the words came from that made them meaningful. He told me to believe in myself and said from every setback there is a comeback, and that I should continue making sure I was ready when my moment came. Now whenever we see each other at games we chat. For someone as big as Mark to take time out of his life to check in on me, and to help me out when we'd never met, really meant a lot. It's something I'll always hold onto. Just knowing I have him in my corner whenever I need him for whatever reason is really special. He's done so much for the game and for goalkeepers. He's a legend in Australia and in England. I'd like to leave the game as he did – so who better to get advice from?

So when the Cup of Nations rolled around, I had sort of flicked this switch and was ready to go. I didn't suspect I would actually be playing until I was the first goalkeeper to arrive in camp. Lyds had a later club game than me so flew from Europe a little later and Teagan was recovering from a concussion. It didn't take a genius to put two and two together, once you considered training and recovery from travel and everything. But informed by my international career until that point, I felt sure it would be the only game of the three I would play. I figured I had nothing to lose and was still a little high from being awarded player of the match in my most recent West Ham game against Arsenal. I was over having complicated feelings about everything, so just decided to take the match as it came. My brother and my niece had come down to Gosford to surprise me and the whole night just felt fun and pressure-free. We defeated Czechia 4–0. I hadn't actually enjoyed a game for the national team in a long while and it was a feeling I relished.

I figured I wouldn't be playing the next game in Sydney because it was against Spain – even if half their team had staged a mutiny and weren't available. But I consciously got out of that mindset of making assumptions about every-thing and just opened myself up to being disappointed. I knew I had played well in the first game and I knew I was having a good season. So if Tony G. didn't pick me, he didn't pick me – that's on him. Well, he picked me. Somebody asked me at the time if I was worried because of what had happened the last time I played Spain. But I had actually forgotten. I don't really tie my performances to an opponent; each one exists in a vacuum. A team is a team – they're still shooting at the same goal. We ended up beating Spain 3–2, wearing rainbow numbers on our jerseys – the first time an Australian national football team had partici-pated in a Pride initiative during an international fixture. And three days after that, I was in goal again when we saw off Jamaica 3–0 in Newcastle.

I was awarded player of the tournament and rose from Australia's no. 3 keeper to its no. 1. The spot was seem-ingly now mine to lose. I just couldn't wrap my head around the fact I had actually had fun. That had never happened to me before. It almost felt like all of the iden-tity crises I had grappled with for so long evaporated into thin air. I was allowed to be myself. To enjoy myself and my friends. To be silly and to back it up on the field. Because I was actually being put on the field. I went to recovery the mornings after matches instead of training. I didn't come on at half-time or only play the easy games. Each time my name appeared on the team sheet, I put another run on the board. Externally, I tried to stay pretty calm, but internally it was a different story. We were five months out from the World Cup and the train seemed to be gathering steam at just the right time.

TONY FRANKEN

Given Lydia and Teagan's unavailability for the opening match, I told the technical staff this had to be her opportunity. I told Macca basically the same. As it happened, she got player of the tournament. She was outstanding. I think that was the turning point for her, the moment she realised that she belonged at that level. The things she did were the things we had been after for a long time from our female goalkeepers. I said to her, 'Well, now you've set the standard. That's what I expect. You've shown you can do it. You played against Spain and you're not going to play against anyone harder than Spain. So what's there to worry about? Go and enjoy, and play.'

In April, we played friendlies against Scotland and England in London and I started both of those games, too. We lost the first 1–0, with Kirsty sitting on the opponents' bench, but I didn't feel the same sense of dread that used to come with defeat while I was in goal. We had lost but I had also played well, and I just knew I would be selected to face England. Two days before the game, I injured myself going down for a save. The impact pushed my forearm back at a gross angle and strained the ligaments on the inside of my elbow. I was in bits. But Teagan was injured again, which left only Lydia, and there was something about her body language that was a little off. That was all I needed to crystallise the fact I was feeling the opposite. I wanted to play, really badly. That night, I could barely move my arm and it was starting to swell; we iced it and it settled down the next day. Medical staff asked me how it felt. I simply said, 'I'm definitely playing this game.' So the physio strapped it up pretty heavily and I was just so focused I didn't feel it once. We beat the reigning European champions 2–0. I felt needed.

The England game also marked the start of a new habit: chewing caffeine gum before games. Caffeine gum is one of the options made available to players for a quick pre-match boost. For some reason, I decided to give it a go on this particular day. It isn't as bad as it sounds – just a little tougher than regular chewing gum. Dad, who was getting ready to watch on TV back home, texted me before the game. 'Are you starting?' he wrote. I replied, 'Yeah, starting. Strained some ligaments in my elbow two days ago. I didn't train yesterday but they've given me until this morning and I've just had a mini-session and got through it. They're just going to tape the shit out of it.' He then messaged, 'Okay, good luck. You'll need to keep up with the chewing gum and you'll be fine.' It was obviously something he had noticed. It quickly became a mental thing, getting me in the zone and focusing my thinking.

17.
Listen and Learn

I didn't properly investigate the gnawing possibility I might have significant hearing loss until almost 29 years after I was tested as a newborn, those results showing my hearing was neither 100 per cent nor bad enough to really worry about. It was about a decade after friends started regularly mentioning they often had to repeat themselves to keep me up to speed in social settings and two and a half years after I realised I had spent a lot of my life lip-reading. It's not that I was in complete denial; it was more a mix of compartmentalisation and ignorant bliss – until, that is, a global pandemic put every face on earth behind a surgical mask and removed my ability to translate visual signals into the meaning their muffled sounds represent. Even before COVID-19, Cait used to cover her mouth sometimes as a joke because she could see me watching her lips move. Instead of taking her point, I'd laugh and tell her to stop being a dickhead then file the issue away again.

When I finally sought and received a diagnosis in October 2022, it made sense genetically. My brother's hearing loss, while much more severe than mine, was diagnosed at two years and nine months, because his speech was indecipherable. He was fitted with hearing aids and underwent intense speech therapy. At school his teachers attached a little microphone to their collar that broadcast straight into his hearing aids to help him learn in a noisy classroom. Because of Sam's impairment, my ears were checked every six months until I was two and then yearly until I was six. The tests found things were overall fine but I do wonder in hindsight if having to work harder than most to hear played a role in my tendency to lose interest so easily during school lessons; if, perhaps, I couldn't quite keep up with the teacher so started my own, less academic conversations with peers instead. I might have just been a bit naughty but I don't remember feeling like one of those kids who is loud and obnoxious just for the sake of it.

SAM ARNOLD

I think it was in her late teenage years that I noticed Kenz would say, 'Huh?' a fair bit. It was almost one of those things that Mum or Dad would correct, as if it was a problem with her manners. But from that point on, it got progressively more obvious to other people.

CAITLIN FOORD

I used to room with Macca and by the end of the camp I wanted to kill her – she was always asking me to repeat myself. I warned her that I would only repeat myself once and if she didn't hear it after that, I was just not going to tell her. But then we would be sitting with the girls around the dinner table, jokes flying around and everyone talking over the top of each other and laughing. And Mac would be sitting next to me asking me what was said or to retell the joke. By the time I would tell her, the joke was gone and the conversation had moved on. It was sad that she just couldn't keep up to speed with it – especially with her FOMO. We tried to tell her so many times that her world would be so different if she could hear properly. She'd just say she wasn't deaf and did not want to wear hearing aids. I guess she was in denial about it or looking for excuses. Even back when we were all in Perth together, I suggested she get her ears checked. And she was like, 'No, I just need to get them cleaned.'

ALANNA KENNEDY

While we were in Perth, Mac said she was going to the GP to check if her ears needed a clean-out. I went along for moral support and sat in the room with her while the doctor examined her ears. It took literally two seconds for him to declare that her ears were perfectly clean. This two-minute appointment was going to cost Mac about $100. At the time, that was a lot of money for us, so I thought I might as well ask him to check my ears as well. He did and then told us my ears were 'reasonably clean' but not as clean as Mac's. We were laughing so much as we left, because Mac had to pay $100 and I got more out of the appointment. We actually did ear candling after that as well – my ears obviously needed a clean.

The girls tried to tell me over and over for years but it was something I just sort of brushed off. Even during COVID, when face masks stopped me from understanding so much, I let it slide. The tipping point for me was probably when Kirst and I got together, because she's so softly spoken. Sometimes I could barely hear her and she had to repeat herself all the time. I remember we once went for a coffee and Kirsty ordered the coffees through a speaker system. When the cashier spoke back through her speaker, it just sounded like a whole heap of words jumbled together. I couldn't make sense of any of it. But Kirsty had understood it perfectly. That was probably the moment for me. I rang Sam on the way to training one morning and said it out loud, 'I think I need to have my hearing checked.' Even though Sam has completely normalised wearing hearing aids in our family, it was confronting. I ran through my symptoms with him on the phone.

SAM ARNOLD

I remember the phone call with Kenz, when she asked if I found it hard to understand people wearing a face mask. I said, 'Yeah, mate. It's a mission.' She agreed. I said, 'Look, how about I do some digging and see if I can find an audiologist in London for you to have some tests?'

It helped so much, because he knew exactly what to look for and removed an extra obstacle from the process. I booked an appointment, expecting to have my ears checked and then just walk out. Case closed. I told the audiologist about our family history and that I lip-read a lot and struggle in loud environments where there's a lot of background noise. I also told her I feel overwhelmed when somebody is talking to me while the TV is on at the same time. Then I sat inside this little booth with headphones on and had to press a button whenever I heard a sound as it shifted through different frequencies. Once it finished and I walked out, I sat down with her at a computer screen. It showed a graph with two lines that looked pretty normal and a third line that dropped well below the others. She told me I have high-frequency hearing loss, or words to that effect. I hardly remember that bit, because I was waiting for what came next: I would definitely need hearing aids. I also learned that the muscles inside your ear deteriorate further over time if you don't wear hearing aids, because they aren't being stimulated enough.

I think she realised it was a lot to take in, because she stopped and asked how I was feeling. As soon as she said it, I burst into tears. I knew deep down it had been a long time coming; it was just a lot of reality hitting all at once. It was also a bit of a relief to finally know for sure. We talked some more about the various hearing-aid options and I left to head home. On the way, I FaceTimed Lans and Cait and was crying so much I couldn't even tell them why I'd called. I kept trying to get it out and they grew increasingly worried I was about to tell them something terrible. When I eventually blurted out that I needed hearing aids, one of them started laughing and said, 'Thank God. We thought maybe someone had died.' They both said they were so proud of me. I went home to Kirst and had another cry, then called family back home. It was just a big, overwhelming day.

ALANNA KENNEDY

She wrote in our group chat, 'Are you guys good for a call?' I was thinking, 'Have we arranged a call and I've forgotten?' Caitlin replied that she was and then Mac started ringing straight away. I saw her face and she was hysterical, to the point I thought, 'Holy shit. Someone's died.' My heart sank. I said, 'Babe, what's going on?' She replied that she needed to get hearing aids. I was so relieved. It was actually really sweet – she was so fucking sad but Cait and I were stoked for her. Her big insecurity was that she was self-conscious about people seeing them but you can hardly see them at all these days. And who cares? She has the capacity to help so many other people who have the same issue and don't want to get their ears checked. They're going to see someone they look up to wearing them and being confident with it.

SAM ARNOLD

When she first told me she needed hearing aids, I could feel the hesitation in her voice about going to the next step. I just said, 'Kenz, the worst-case scenario is you don't wear them. So just get them and suss it out. And you've got to remember when you first get them, it's going to be so uncomfortable. Some of the noises that you hear will annoy you, because the sounds are amplified. The initialisation feels loud, almost ridiculous. But then, over a period of time, your ears will adjust and you will just stop noticing.'

There can be a bit of self-consciousness around how people will perceive you. Hearing aids are not quite as accepted as, say, a pair of glasses. During my early years at school, I was so self-conscious about it and was always the butt of some joke. It gave me a thicker skin and taught me not to take things personally, but I could see the cogs turning in Kenz's mind. I tried to get her to look past that feeling and realise she had a public profile. She had a platform that could elicit empathy and help her transition.

After that, I moved forward pretty quickly. Kirsty came with me to have the hearing aids fitted about 10 days later, before I went away for international friendlies against Scotland and England, and when I returned we went to pick them up. Just before I put the hearing aids in for the first time, Kirsty asked me if I could hear the rain outside. I couldn't. As soon as they were in, I could. In hindsight, it was mad that I couldn't hear things like that but I obviously didn't even think twice about it. The next day, we went for a walk together and I could hear this jingling sound but couldn't work out what it was. Eventually, I asked Kirst and she said it was just our keys moving around in her pocket. A couple of days after that, we went out for dinner and I used the background noise in the restaurant to play around with the settings on the app the hearing aids come with. You can adjust the volume and focus on either what's right in front of you or take in noises further afield. The biggest new thing was music – I could hear the lyrics properly! The whole thing was just unreal. My hearing aids also have Bluetooth, so my Spotify can play through them and phone calls come through to them. I ended up with the same kind as my brother and we have spent a bit of time comparing.

CAITLIN FOORD

I noticed straight away when I met her in London for breakfast. It was the first time I had seen her with her hearing aids and I didn't have to repeat myself once. Even in the noisy café, she wasn't looking at my lips. I gave her so much positive reinforcement about that at the time because the difference was night and day. It was just so nice. I even tried her hearing aids. Obviously, because I don't need them, it just sounded like a buzz in my ear – as if I was in a tunnel and everything was echoing.

I was living with Grace Fisk at the time and even her girl-friend noticed, telling Grace it was so much easier now to chill on the couch and have a chat. It was crazy how much other people were reacting.

Kirsty filmed me picking them up. At the time, she did it with the intention of sending it to my family – because it was a big day and would be nice to have. We ended up having it edited and I posted it on Instagram. It was a cool video but I also thought that, by proactively putting my news out into the world, I might not have to deal with the attention every time someone new noticed them. I figured if everyone could see straight away, it would be done. 'Those closest to me know how long I've avoided this day, but here's a little glimpse of a life-changing day for me,' I wrote. 'Yesterday I picked up my hearing aids, and although it's something I'll need to get used to, I couldn't be more grateful for this little adjustment.' I did not predict the response. I received messages from so many parents and kids, and other adults in my position who had also avoided the reality of hearing loss. I still get feedback from the public to this day.

Just after Christmas in 2023, I was with my family in Lennox Head and this mum approached me in a random shopping centre and thanked me for being a role model to her children. She herself had a proper cochlear implant. In February 2024, a couple of girls with hearing aids came to our win over Arsenal just to meet me and thank me. I guess no one really had a role model with hearing loss in sport. I had Sam but most people go through it on their own. Now I have a partnership with Audika. They retested my hearing again in Australia and fitted me with another pair.

I had already made the decision that I wasn't going to wear my hearing aids during training and games, especially given how precarious my starting position felt. I didn't want any big changes that could distract me and prompt a mistake. I've since trained a few times in the ones I wear now but I don't know if I'll ever wear them during games. The hearing loss doesn't affect me much when playing. I am doing a lot of the talking rather than the other way around and there's no way I would be able to hear someone from the sideline over a crowd of 50,000, even if I was wearing them.

18.
In the Zone

Before most major tournaments, club and country engage in a predictable dance around player ownership. In the case of the WSL during the weeks before the 2023 World Cup, clubs were advocating for a post-season break so we didn't burn out. National teams, conversely, were eager for us to start training together as soon as humanly possible. This push and pull was par for the course and occurred particularly in places where domestic leagues had just finished and player welfare is more critical. West Ham had endured a torrid end to our 2022–23 campaign, losing 4–0 to Manchester United in March, 6–2 to Manchester City in April and 4–0 to Chelsea in May. On top of that, our manager Paul Konchesky – who had been elevated from assistant after Olli Harder resigned at the end of the previous season – was sacked. Shit was hitting the fan on the staff side. While I was thrilled to be named players' player of the season, Kirst and I were mentally exhausted.

Scotland hadn't qualified for the World Cup, so Kirst was done for the season, and West Ham agreed with the Matildas I would have a three-week break before joining camp. I knew I needed some time away to reset mentally, so we went to Greece for 10 days. We stayed in Rhodes and Kirsty's parents joined us for the last few days of the trip. It was a proper rest with no training. We kept active by playing tennis and I did two strength sessions to keep my muscles activated so I wouldn't suffer from soreness after the first session back in camp. The fear of starting my World Cup preparations underdone and losing my starting spot was what drove me in the end to cut my holiday short.

Pre-camp was on the Gold Coast, so I flew in a week ahead of schedule and was one of the first to arrive in Australian camp. It felt good to be back, ticking off each session and getting my body and mind ready to hit the ground running once everyone else arrived. West Ham ideally wanted me to have more of a break but I wanted to get back into training as I felt it gave me an edge, and also showed Tony G. and Tony F. that I was committed and wanted it. It was nice, as well, to be able to have dinner with my parents or go and see my brother and his kids.

When the rest of the girls arrived, I moved into the team hotel on the Gold Coast. We were there for about three weeks all up, building towards our pre-tournament friendly against France in Melbourne. During that time, the Matildas tried to make everything feel as normal as possible, as if we were gathered for a run-of-the-mill training camp and not a home World Cup. They gave us weekends off and allowed us to go home and see family. Some girls flew interstate for a couple of days. I obviously didn't have very far to travel, which made my life easier. But it also counterintuitively had the effect of making me feel a little stretched. Because I was so close to my family geographically, I spent every spare minute I had with them. If we had a spare hour to rest in our hotel room, I would go for a visit instead. If training started later one day, I'd squeeze in breakfast with Mum. I was on the go non-stop without realising it, pulling myself in too many directions. My family didn't pressure me to do this – quite the opposite. It just happened that way. It wasn't until we had landed in Melbourne that Tony F. suggested I might have been feeling a bit overwhelmed. He told me about one of the Socceroos he had worked with who competed in his home city and had to tell his family he just needed to be on his own in camp, because all they wanted to do was see him. Tony made it clear I was still training well, just noted a change in mindset since boarding the flight, almost as if I had clicked properly into World Cup mode. The Gold Coast had been so much fun and I took the girls to my favourite sushi place and some good brunch spots, and to the beach. But Melbourne was when I really felt I could focus on what we were there to do.

I wouldn't say I was overly confident. But I certainly felt that I belonged more and my teammates must have noticed. I have since seen interviews with some of the more experienced girls, such as Polks and Lyds, who both said they saw me coming into my own during this period.

I felt more at ease with Tony G., too. I no longer dreaded interacting with him or tried to present a version of myself I believed he wanted to see. I stopped trying to read his mind and started to see his questions about my season with West Ham as genuine. He even asked me questions about where he should eat and get his coffee on the Gold Coast and I put together a list for him and Jens Fjellström, our assistant coach. These nice social exchanges, small as they were, would never have occurred in the past. In hindsight, I realise that is probably partly because I avoided them, thinking that, because I hadn't proved myself on the field, talking to him off it would be wasting his time. Now I felt I could put myself out there a bit more without fear of rejection.

I was also, by this point, pretty certain I would be selected in the squad. FIFA allows for 23 players in World Cup squads – five more than a non-COVID Olympics – and almost all head coaches select three goalkeepers. Even if I wasn't certain I'd be actually playing, I knew I was in the top three. My place in the squad was confirmed towards the end of pre-camp, in a slightly unorthodox way. In a meeting after training one day, Tony G. posted two groups of names on the board. Each group was to meet separately back at the meeting room later in the afternoon for a walk-through session of set plays and that sort of thing. I was grouped with several core players, including Sam, Steph, Caitlin, Ellie, Alanna, Hayley, Mini, Emily, Lydia, Polks and Tameka – players who had been with the national team for a long time. The other group was made up of effectively the rest of the extended squad. This wasn't really unusual in itself. So we went down at our allotted time and then completed the walk-throughs. Once we were back in the room and sitting in a circle, Tony says, out of the blue, 'I just want to let you guys know now that you have been selected for the World Cup.' It was a little bit awkward because we all just sort of sat there and looked at each other like, 'What now?' So we offered mutual congratulations and made a bigger deal out of Lyds and Polks because it was going to be their fifth World Cup. Most of us in the room at that time knew we would probably make the cut; it just felt unusual to have us all together like that. I don't know why Tony did it this way but can only assume he thought it might have been nice because we all sort of grew up together and knew each other so well.

The other factor was that he wouldn't have had time to meet with every single player individually and it likely made more sense to have those individual meetings with less experienced players, who were either being cut or potentially making the squad for their first World Cup. I understood both of these reasons and have to acknowledge that my feelings around this are in no way Tony's responsibility. But I admit to feeling a little envious about some of the other girls' selection moments, especially after seeing the videos posted on social media. My last selection moment was being cut from the Olympic team and I thought this might have been a nice time for a one-on-one conversation to recognise how much things have turned around for me since then. Even though this would technically have been my third World Cup, it still felt like my first, because I hadn't yet made my World Cup debut. But I guess I was late to the party and couldn't expect coaches to always wait for me to rock up. I was in and that's what counted most.

Tony asked us as a group to keep our selection quiet until the following day, when the rest of the meetings would be happening. That was pretty straightforward at dinner that evening, in the sense that we had completed our walk-throughs and there was nothing more to say. It became more difficult the following morning, when the others were given time slots and began to enquire about ours. I felt like I had to fudge it and say I hadn't been given one yet or wasn't sure. All we could do after that was be there for those who were cut. It was really sad for Chloe Logarzo and Emily Gielnik, who were both trying to come back from injuries and are important members of the squad. But the worst for me to watch was Remy Siemsen. We're all quite close with Remy and have known her since she was young. She always works really hard. We were rooting for her. Kyah was selected over Remy as the last forward. I could see both sides to that decision. Kyah has been a phenomenal player for the Matildas over the years and she was looking good in pre-camp, which is an achievement in itself considering she had ruptured her ACL eight months prior, in October. I think I just knew how badly Remy wanted it.

On the whole, pre-camp was a blast and had some nice touches. One of my most treasured souvenirs is the

Love Island water bottle we were each given. We would each walk around with them – and I still have an embarrassing number of *Love Island*-water-bottle selfies on my phone. Alanna and I know every single contestant from every season, we were that obsessed. But I would sacrifice that water bottle for another visit from Cathy Freeman. While in Melbourne, two nights before our warm-up friendly against France, Tony G. scheduled a team meeting for 6:30 p.m. We assumed it would be another tactics session to dot our i's and cross our t's. But once we were all seated, he turned off the lights, then a big screen at the front of the room lit up with Cathy's gold medal-winning 400-metre sprint at the Sydney 2000 Olympics. Do you know what the most beautifully jarring thing about this was? I didn't previously have much of an affinity with this as an iconic sporting moment. I was six years old when Cathy ran that race, and it's difficult to attribute meaning to an event I didn't really witness in real time. But as I was watching this three-minute highlights reel, it suddenly felt significant. When the lights turned back on and Cathy herself was standing in the same room – and after we all looked at each other and silently exclaimed, 'Holy shit,' to anybody looking – I got it. I could fathom the effect her performance that day had on Australian sporting and cultural history at the time and for the subsequent 23 years. For a few minutes, that translated into a feeling of expectation on us as a team to do something our country could be proud of. But then Cathy sat with us and talked about the lead-up to that race and described the lack of pressure she actually felt. She said she had done everything she needed to do to prepare and knew before she was even on the starting blocks that she was going to win. There was something about hearing her say she didn't feel any pressure that made my own nerves evaporate. When she recounted how she used the crowd at Stadium Australia to her advantage, I felt we could do that in our opening match, too, against the Republic of Ireland. She was so humble and so human, and what she said resonated so much with me. I know it did even more so with Sam, who has idolised her for a long time, and with Lydia and Kyah because of their First Nations connection. Cathy had dinner with us in the meal room that evening and we all just had a chat. The whole thing was surreal and in many ways added the final touches to our preparation.

19.
Up for the Cup

We were on the eve of a home World Cup but the buzz hadn't yet arrived. Sure, there was some media present and people recognised Sam on the street. But the rest of us? Not so much. During pre-camp, we got into our hotel lift one morning en route back from training and another guest got in at another floor going up. The person looked at our uniforms and asked if we were netballers. No, mate. We are literally about to play at a FIFA World Cup. It was hilarious. I was still virtually unrecognisable to the public and will concede I was more than fine with that because I could focus on myself with minimal interruptions. I wanted to be in goal for that opening group game against Ireland and I knew Tony G. would almost certainly start his preferred goalkeeper in the warm-up against France.

I was named, which of course meant my anxiety transferred from 'I have to be selected' to 'I need to play well and clear this final hurdle'. I was pretty nervous walking out at Marvel Stadium on 14 July. The whole

Cathy-Freeman-didn't-feel-the-pressure-so-I-won't-either motto went out the window. I was suddenly back at the Cup of Nations with no runs on the board and trying to prove myself all over again. Add to that the fact that my whole family was in the stands with the other 50,000 spectators. So was Kirsty, who had flown out with her dad to watch.

The opening 16 minutes of the match felt so weird. I remember making a couple of passes but mostly slipping briefly back into the old mindset. Telling myself that I must not make a mistake. Whenever I touched the ball, I thought, 'Don't fuck it up.' Then, in the 17th minute, Selma Bacha swooped in and rifled a powerful shot towards our goal. I took it on the chest and as soon as I'd made that save, I was back in the present. Back in game mode and up and about. Able to recognise that feeling belonged to the old me and that I didn't need to be held back by her anymore. I suppose this is why warm-up friendlies exist; to help us shake out the nerves before everything gets real. Mary Fowler ensured we won, coming off the bench after half-time to score off a cutback from Hayley Raso. That was when people started noticing her habit of wearing black gloves while playing – the first of many idiosyncrasies within the team that would become the source of public curiosity. After that game, nobody mistook us for netballers again.

In our goalkeeping review, Tony F. asked me how I felt and I confessed to feeling nervous early on. He said he could see that but felt that as soon as I made that first save I was right as rain. I wondered if that was obvious to everybody or just to Tony because he seems to know how I am feeling and when I am feeling it. Either way, I had been given a taste of World Cup football and wanted more. The crowd radiated a buoyant quality I had never experienced from on the field before. I was still second-guessing whether I would play in the tournament proper but I figured I had moved to about a 70 per cent probability. Though I never said that out loud in case I jinxed myself.

The day after that game in Melbourne, we flew to Brisbane, where we would set up camp for the entirety of the group stage. Each nation is permitted to create a home away from home at their accommodation somewhere in the tournament's host country or countries, with all the personal touches they need to help them perform (once the knockout stages commence, FIFA dictates venues and hotels depending on how the draw pans out). This was the first time the 'base camp' concept had been included at a Women's World Cup – the plan for Australia was to train at the Queensland Sport and Athletics Centre and stay at Rydges South Bank. On match day minus one, we would fly to the city hosting our game, stay for two nights and fly back to Brisbane the day after each game. We had Ireland in Sydney on 20 July, then we remained in Brisbane to face Nigeria on 27 July before travelling to Melbourne for the final group match against Canada on 31 July.

In terms of our digs, Football Australia did not disappoint. Staff had decked out Rydges with everything imaginable to make it welcoming and fun. Each of our rooms had individualised name plates fixed to the door and do-not-disturb signs that read 'Tired Tilly'. We also had personalised doormats and pillows, and FA had framed special collages on our tables using photos secretly sent over by our families. Mini's mum even arranged for flowers to be sent to all of our rooms. But it was everything outside of our rooms as well. Green and gold covered the hallways. When we went to the lunch room, we were literally staring at giant murals of ourselves. We had a barista privately drafted in – the same one who made coffee for the Socceroos at the 2022 men's World Cup in Qatar. It *felt* as if we were entering the World Cup.

It was important, because we were used to seeing each other in hotels all the time. Another stock-standard hotel would have made this just another Matildas camp. But *this* was a World Cup. Before this, we had never really had a proper common room before either. At other hotels for past tournaments, there were sometimes beanbags and some other little bits and pieces but never enough to coax us all out of our rooms. This common room was a dead-set lounge room on steroids. It had big, comfy couches with blankets and a big television on one side, and recliner chairs and bean bags on the other. And there was a ping-pong table and a craft table with beading, colouring-in supplies and Lego. Sometimes Mini would be there with her little girl Harper.

We spent every damn minute on those couches, glued to whatever group game was happening at the time. Even though everybody had a TV in their room, we all sat together for most of our spare time. Someone would post in the group WhatsApp chat: 'Meet you at the TV room,' or, 'Meet you at the couch,' and before you knew it, five of us would be there and our chef Vini would be cooking up a snack. We generally trained in the morning then settled in for an afternoon or evening of fixtures. I would say Steph and I were the most keen. Sam and Hayley and Ellie joined us quite a bit, and Lans and Cait came every now and then, too. The latter pair were mainly my sticker-book partners in crime. We were obsessed with the 2023 Women's World Cup sticker books and spent hours opening and sorting player cards to try to fill our albums. When we first received them, we set up down one end of the hallway. Sam and Steph were in the end rooms opposite each other and Caitlin and I were right next to them, so we commandeered the whole end of the hallway and went to town. Whenever Sam and Steph tried to get in or out of their rooms, they had an obstacle course to navigate. We traded cards. Alanna jokingly got annoyed because she was given some doubles. It didn't take much to amuse us.

We also received a near-constant stream of cool gifts from sponsors. Ellie got us each an Xbox Series S through an arrangement she had with Microsoft and I got my first World Cup box from Nike. We got one from Frank Green, too. Reminder after reminder that it was getting close to go time.

Our final training session came and went, and I rode a rollercoaster of emotions as I started in goal for part of the session, before Tony G. swapped us out. I know I should have remembered I had done enough to be there but even when we all crowded in for the night-time meeting and the PowerPoint went up, I was still only about 90 per cent sure. I just had all these potential scenarios whirling around and I thought at any point he could turn around and be like, 'Oops, joke's on you.' When, after all that, my name popped up, I was so relieved.

LYDIA WILLIAMS

I've had a long time – and I'm talking years – to accept that my role now is one of mentorship. To offer support to whoever is ready. It took me a long time to get there. But definitely by 2020–21 I was in that space of finding my fulfilment through the team winning and the team doing really well, and making sure that whoever was playing in goals – if it wasn't me – had the most support they could have from me. When Mac did what she did at the World Cup, I was so proud. She's been behind and watched me play for so long; the World Cup felt like a little handover.

I have had the best relationship with Lydia through everything, because we've always understood where each other is. It's hard for me to remember now because I feel like whenever I was in that weird transition with her, she was injured or she was competing with Bubs or I got injured or dropped. There was never direct competition between us and she was never dropped for me. So we were always learning from each other and having conversations. She'd told me countless times that when she left, she wanted me to wear her no. 1 jersey. All us goalkeepers want is to wear the no. 1 jersey so for Lyds to have passed it on to me when she announced her international retirement was the pinnacle for me.

Lydia presented the jersey to me in front of the whole team in the meal room during a camp in May 2024. 'When you walk into a changeroom, the first thing you see is where your number is,' she said. 'It's how you identify yourself. It's something that is a part of you. It's just as important as a signature. And the beauty about sport and what this team is, is that numbers are meant to be passed on.' She looked at me, then, and the moment felt so overwhelming I started to cry. I got up and gave her a hug, and then took a moment to compose myself before I was able to speak.

'Obviously when I first came into camp, it wasn't my most ideal camp,' I said. 'As we all know, there was a bit of up and down. But I remember coming in and watching you and Bubs battle it out for this jersey. And I remember watching you take it and become your own. I knew from that moment that this was what I eventually wanted to wear. We've gone through a lot, and I know that I probably couldn't have kept going and got to this place without you. So to take this from you means more than you know. Congratulations on such an amazing career, and I'm so glad that I could be a part of it.'

Lydia had for so long been the image of goalkeeping for the Matildas, and the face of many of our causes. It feels crazy to think about my new parallel reality.

20.
Game 1, Ireland

To the general public, Sam Kerr was the face of this World Cup. To us, she was our captain and our friend. Those two labels were front and centre when she broke the news she was injured on the morning of the match. Unbeknownst to us, she'd had scans the previous afternoon and the results had returned a calf injury that would likely keep her out for the entire group stage. Sam and Tony G. had put on their best poker faces at the previous evening's press conference and fooled the world – and, most importantly, Ireland – into believing our star striker was fit as a fiddle and ready to go. The next morning, when she gathered us in a circle at our accommodation and brought us up to date, half the team were crying. We needed her on the pitch but we were also just so sad for her. Three years of build-up and keeping herself fit, only to be sidelined the day before the main event. What a kick in the guts.

There are more than 600 muscles in the human body; some experts suggest this number is closer to 800. When all are in working order, they comprise the body of one of the world's most prolific goalscorers. When a single one – albeit a sizeable one (Sam did joke she has 'the biggest calves in the world') – is out of order, that entire body is rendered unusable on a football pitch. The sum on its own feels unfair. On a personal level for me, it changed a key part of my routine.

When a team walks out of the tunnel to play a match, the captain goes first and the goalkeeper second. For every match I had started in 2023, Sam had walked out directly in front of me and stood next to me for the national anthems. Having her with me in the tunnel calmed me down. Sam is very lighthearted when we're waiting to walk out, so the two of us would always joke around and have a laugh. It sounds like a small thing but that chit-chat kept me from thinking too much about what was to come and what was at stake. When I start to think too much, I freak out and can psych myself out of playing well.

This would be the first time she wasn't there. Back in my room while trying to rest, I couldn't stop thinking about this. In the end, I texted Sam. 'I feel so lame writing this but I don't want to make a big deal out of it at the game,' I wrote. 'I'm going to get you to write "SK20" on some tape on my wrist for the game, just because you've been with me in every game that I've played this year and have really brought out the confidence in me out on the field, so it wouldn't feel right without you beside me tonight. Don't make this weird. You're still a loser but I need you for this one.' Sam replied, 'This makes me cry. Thanks, Mac.

You're going to fucking crush it tonight and I can't wait to watch you. Love you, my friend.' Even if she couldn't physically be by my side, I could still, in my own way, carry her with me. It was a curveball but one I could deal with.

I have a bit of a game-day routine, though it isn't hard and fast. I've naturally adapted it over the years as I discovered what I like and don't like, and that night's 8 p.m. kick-off dictated that the day followed the pattern I adopted for late games. I wake up about 8:30 a.m. – I set my alarm for later but rarely sleep until then. If we are in Australia and my parents have come to watch, I meet them for breakfast at a café near our hotel (this particular morning, I had breakfast with Kirsty and her dad) and eat something simple such as avocado and poached eggs on toast with a skinny flat white. At about 11:30, we head out for our team walk; I take a bottle of water with a dissolved Hydralyte tablet. When we return, I do stretching and mobility and head straight from there to lunch. I eat a sandwich or wrap with ham and salad, and a yoghurt. Early afternoon is time for rest and I hang in my room from 1 p.m. until 3:30 p.m. Sometimes I just chill out in bed and watch something on my iPad; other times I might have a nap. At about 4 p.m., we all meet in the meal room for a pre-match meal and I usually have a bowl of pasta with a tomato-based sauce (nothing creamy or too heavy). Then I go back to my room to shower and dress. While there, I straighten my hair, do my make-up and pack my bag. All up, getting ready takes me about 90 minutes. I take my bag to the pre-game team meeting, at which we are given last messages from the coaches. Then we all hop straight on the bus to head to the stadium. I put my earbuds in and listen to music – whatever comes up on my playlist but it is always chilled-out stuff.

It was on the bus that the enormity of what was coming began to descend on me. I had played it cool with Kirsty that morning, acting as if this was just any old game. I'd even played it cool with myself, almost convincing myself this was just another friendly. We played Ireland less than two years ago – we're just doing that again. When footballers say, 'One game at a time,' that is mostly for our own benefit. We aren't pretending to the public that we haven't looked at the draw and worked out all the possible scenarios – of course we have. But most of the time, we are attempting to block out every scenario except the one right in front of us: the game we must play here and now.

As the bus makes the turn-off to Olympic Park, and my exercise of reimagining our World Cup opener into a meaningless friendly starts to feel unfeasible, I text Kirsty. 'I'm nervous,' I write. At first, I regret putting the admission in writing, as if saying it makes it real and therefore the source of more stress. But there is already so much stress as it is. And after a few seconds, after re-reading the words on the screen, they feel better in Kirsty's safekeeping. I couldn't exactly drop that on a teammate – everybody else is going through their own process. Making their own bargains with themselves, texting the people they need to text, listening to the songs they need to hear. Twenty-three silent girls on a bus with crescendoing thoughts.

We arrive at the ground at about 6 p.m. When you drive into the bowels of a stadium, you miss most of the outside spectacle. The more punctual fans lining up to buy merchandise or drinking beers at the bar. The mass influx from the train station at 15-minute intervals. The hot chips and hamburgers and new Matildas jerseys and old Socceroos jerseys, and the fans with signs.

We chart a clean path around and then underneath all of it, into the dark underground and back entrances where the only people present have official accreditation lanyards around their necks. This is the final assembly before the main event and I like to take my time.

When we enter our changeroom some players get dressed into their kit immediately and others head straight for the physio. Everyone has their regimen and habits and order of operation. My main objective is to avoid having to wait around once I am ready. Waiting invites thinking and thinking isn't something I like to do too early before a game. So I often sit in my locker for 10–15 minutes, just looking around and getting my bearings. Set myself up for a calm evening. Only once I feel in control of myself do I begin to get ready. I take off my jewellery then put on my warm-up shirt and playing shorts and socks, and head for the player bathrooms to redo my hair. If the hair is good, I just add hairspray to hold it in place.

Then I go to see the physio. I have my elbow strapped before each World Cup game because I'd injured it at our previous camp in England, so I take 10 minutes to sit down with our physio, Pete, and chat as he wraps the sections of arm below and above my right elbow. He adds some tape to my right wrist as well. I take my time walking back. There is always so much time. I stretch it out with Alanna, singing and dancing around and being silly to a song that's started up. Kyah, now sidelined again with injury, has become our unofficial DJ, looking after the speakers at training and compiling playlists for different occasions. I'm not into heavy music but a good mix of singalongs and pump-up tunes are good just before a game. The hustle and bustle of everyone getting ready helps as well.

During the flurry, I look up and notice Sam standing over by the coffee machine, on the same side of the changeroom as my locker. She is quietly crying. I walk over to her and give her a hug, which sets me off. She keeps saying, 'I'm fine, I'm fine,' and clearly doesn't want to make a big deal of it. I can tell she doesn't want to let it out because she doesn't want to make it about her, but it must have got to her, seeing all of us getting ready to play such a big game in the knowledge she'd play no part in half of it. Neither of us are overly emotional people and I don't want it to be a thing, so I go back to my locker and sit down. Soon after that, she comes over to me with a marker and writes 'SK20' on my wrist taping. Quiet and matter of fact. I'm not even sure if we exchange words. I give her a quick hug but the moment is understated. I said what I needed to say in my text earlier in the day.

I head for the stretching room, where mats and foam rollers are set up for us to loosen up before we warm up on the pitch. Because goalkeepers usually start the warm-up before the outfield players, we generally complete our dynamic warm-up inside before heading out. Those who have already taken their seats make sounds to suggest they are very happy to see us. This likely contributes to my rise in confidence. As does the fact that the warm-up comes and goes without a hitch. And the fact that I can now say, with 100 per cent certainty, that I am Australia's starting goalkeeper for at least the first match. The nerves subside.

TONY FRANKEN

Mark Schwarzer, in my opinion, was one of the best goalkeepers I ever worked with as a professional. His attention to detail leading into games was second to none. He would want to know everything about what a striker was doing in a training session the day before the game. Mackenzie is a little bit different, in that she wants to be by herself on match day and goes through her normal routine. But one thing both of them have in common is that, once we go out for warm-up, 45 minutes or so prior to the game, there's this focus. And they could be playing in front of three people or 100,000 – it really doesn't matter. Because once the whistle goes, they're oblivious to everything else going on around them.

I always grab them at the end of the warm-up, before they go in the tunnel, just to reinforce some key messaging. It might be just three short phrases – triggers for them to think about. But I look at game day as being their day and try not to say too much. It might be something like, 'Stay high and look for the ball beyond. Defend the space.' Or, 'One minute at a time, one action at a time.' Or, 'Take the crowd in during the anthem but then it's about the game – nothing else matters.' If the opponent has a really dangerous striker, I might say, 'Be aware of her cutting in and shooting.'

Back in the changeroom, we get into our playing shirts and I slip a piece of caffeine gum into my mouth. Then the starting XI walk into the tunnel as a team. When you're standing underneath a stadium full of people, there is a strange texture to the sound – it's both muffled and strong at the same time, if that is possible. If you are on edge while waiting in the tunnel, it sounds like a nightmare. But if you are ready to play, that muted reverberation is enticing.

A crowd of more than 75,000 tempt us towards the light of a mild Sydney winter's night. When the music plays and the time comes, I do not feel overwhelmed. I chat with Steph, positioned directly in front of me as our stand-in captain. This is our opening match and yet there is an odd finality to it. We have all been in camp for an eternity and now we are stepping over the threshold.

After the Welcome to Country, the national anthems play. It might sound trite but this really is a time I think about a lot of things. I fall into this mode of reflection. How I got here, that my family and friends are watching. It feels meaningful. I look over to Sam on the bench and she's crying. My tear ducts started working away, too. The funny thing is that 'Advance Australia Fair' is only about 40 seconds long and as soon as it finishes, I'm done with the sentimentality. I snap straight out of it and am ready to play. Sam joins our huddle and says something very small, but it's Steph who gives the speech as part of her captaincy duties.

*

That match felt so good. We had done our analysis on them, including Denise O'Sullivan and Katie McCabe, whose skills I knew all about from playing Arsenal in the WSL. But I mostly just took them as they came. We had a lot of the ball but it still was a bit of an arm wrestle, until Marissa Sheva brought Hayley down in Ireland's box and we were awarded a penalty. My lasting memory is of Steph converting that penalty, early in the second half, and the craziness of the crowd and our celebrations. I'd never had a feeling like that take over my body before. I'd never seen Steph celebrate like that either. Everyone just went fucking crazy. It got crazier still in the last 20 minutes, which were absolute chaos. Cross after cross came in, resulting in corner after corner. One curled towards the back post and I just got a touch on it to send it out for another corner. When I got up from the fall, Caitlin was standing right in front of me. She chest bumped and yelled, 'Fuck yes, Mac!' She had never been like that on the pitch either. Everyone was just on a different level and it was so sick to be a part of.

The relief when it was over was huge. It wasn't our best performance but it was out of the way. We had been building up to it for so long – beating Ireland dissolved the pressure and allowed us to settle and focus on the rest of the tournament.

Tony F. was stoked for me. I could tell straight away, because he wears a pretty obvious grin when I've played well. And he gave me a big hug. Jens also came up to me, grabbed me by the shoulders and simply said, 'You are such a good goalkeeper.' It was really nice to hear and also a bit funny because I didn't know how to take it. I thanked him and walked away, and then thought, 'Wait, did he just figure that out now by watching that one game?' I knew how he meant it, though – Jens had always made time for me whenever he came to meet other London-based players. He would invite me to make me feel included and he's always been more approachable than Tony G.

Speaking of Tony G., he was quite emotional, though that isn't exactly unusual for him. He looked how we felt and I sensed he was pretty damn happy, if trying to dial it down a bit. We were all just on a high. I knew I would struggle to sleep.

It took ages just to get out of the stadium. I said hi to my family and Kirsty and her dad, and stayed on the pitch to greet fans and do signings. Then I went to shower and change. We do this thing after every match where all coaches and staff leave the changeroom so that it's just us players in there. We sit in our lockers and have a debrief on the match. Just a quick conversation about how we thought the game went. It's very informal and anyone can speak at any point. After that, we jumped on the bus back to the hotel. Following late games, it can be almost midnight by the time you're eating dinner, and it was later still when I left the hotel to see Kirsty at her apartment. She was due to leave Australia two days later as she had to get back to London for the start of West Ham's preseason. It was nice to see her again before a month-long gap.

The next morning, we both went out for breakfast with my whole family, which was so lovely. When I play well, I feel elated for the entirety of the next day. It is one of the few times I have nothing to worry about, which just about makes it my favourite time.

At around lunchtime, we flew back to our base camp in Brisbane and basically spent the afternoon recovering and having massages and saunas, and relaxing in our rooms. The day after that, we had training in the morning and the afternoon off. I went to my brother's to see him, his wife and the kids, and by early evening I was back in the lounge room with the girls watching Japan's 5–0 win over Zambia. Every now and then, Vini would bring us snacks – kind of how your mum brings out snacks while you are watching TV with your friends at home. He even had a popcorn machine. So there we were, eating pita and hummus and watching football while everyone else in the country was losing their minds.

21.
Game 2, Nigeria

Sam's injury had blindsided everyone outside of the Matildas camp and a national debate was raging about the supposed ethics of Tony G. and Sam pretending everything was fine during their pre-match press conference, when they knew she would be sidelined for weeks. Tony had been cagey when asked about the fitness of his players and wider Australia was now sifting through his words with new perspective. I personally agreed with the view of Sydney Roosters coach Trent Robinson. 'The coach's job for Australia is to win the game,' Robinson told media the day after the game. 'And if that was a tactical advantage so Australia could win the game then I think we're happy with that as Australians, rather than having the knowledge hours before that Sam wasn't playing.'

Inside our bubble, though, not much had changed. Sam was doing everything she needed to do rehab-wise and the rest of us were focusing on ourselves. We noticed Sam's absence most at training. That's when the media noticed it the most, too, and the TV cameras and photographers watched her like a hawk for their allotted 15-minute observation window. If Sam sat on a crate, photos of Sam sitting on a crate would be all over the back pages of the next day's newspapers. If Sam iced her calf, the photos would be of Sam icing her calf. Sam would sometimes joke she might ice the other calf just to see what speculation she could start. The amount of coverage was a new level of crazy. Even during our press conferences, so many questions were asked about Sam. We got it, so we copped it, but it did get a little tiresome after a while. We were like, 'Righto. You know the rest of us are still playing a World Cup here?'

And we were, by this point, deep in preparation to play our second group game. We knew a win would seal progression to the round of 16 with a game to spare. Even a draw might be enough, depending on the other result between Ireland and Canada. Two days before the game, Mary and Aivi Luik were both concussed in training. It was so unfortunate but just one of those things. The media picked it up in a big way and ran with it – and there were also a few funny memes. My favourite that did the rounds showed two people running into each with pots on their heads and a caption reading 'Matildas training'. Even after that, we were pretty relaxed. We didn't have Mary up front but Emily was ready to step in. All of that stuff sorts itself out. Weirdly, the thing that made me the most worried was discovering I'd be wearing the pink jersey. The only other time I had worn the pink was the friendly against Scotland and we had lost. I enjoyed the best games wearing black, and purple seemed to be a mixed bag. Of course, that is magical thinking and our performance against Nigeria didn't come down to a shirt colour.

I've retrospectively asked myself whether I was too relaxed. I probably was. I probably mucked around a bit too much and took the result a bit for granted because everything had felt so good after the Ireland win. The game turned bad as soon as Nigeria equalised. Emily opened the scoring in first-half stoppage time and at that point I assumed we would glide through. Five minutes after that, as a stoppage time ticked down, I had a goal kick. Half the girls wanted me to go long and half wanted me to play out. So I passed to Clare Hunt, hoping she would play out. But she passed straight back to me, so I went long. Nigeria were ready and before I knew it Uchenna Kanu had equalised. At half-time, words were flying around everywhere and at pace. The girls were back and forth about what happened with that goal, saying Nigeria should never have scored against us and asking what we were doing. It fed the pressure and the second half descended into a comedy of errors. The worst for me was the miscommunication with Alanna that directly led to Nigeria's third goal. Asisat Oshoala, introduced off the bench, ran onto a ball over the top of our defence. As she did, I came off my line to collect it. But Lans had the same idea and attempted to head the ball back to me. The result was empty space between both of us and our goal – Oshoala pounced on our miscommunication and lofted the ball into the net from a tight angle.

Nothing seemed to go right that entire 90 minutes. Nigeria were very good and we let them make a meal of us. I know I didn't play as well as I could have and it bummed me out. Even Tony G. was going mental on the sideline, when what we really needed was to all chill the fuck out. He said at the end of the game that he might have needed to communicate more clearly and he really copped it publicly for his game management and substitutions. But really, it was all of us. None of us were on the same page. Afterwards, in our player-only locker meeting, we all talked briefly. Lans apologised for her role in Nigeria's third goal. Later, I went straight to her and said it had been as much me as it was her. But we left it there for now – it was still fresh.

During the formal match review with coaches, we all tried to understand where each of us was coming from. And we did. It was just that at that particular point in time, we were all over the place. We went into the game pretty confident, which is not an issue in itself. But we were also a little bit complacent, a tendency against lesser teams. This setback served as a reminder of our inclination to shoot ourselves in the foot sometimes, of the need to always remain focused.

It also had me questioning my starting spot all over again and whether the whole thing might have given Tony G. cause to think about using Teagan or Lydia next time. That habitual defeatism still lurked – the avoidable nature of a couple of my errors against Nigeria let it back out of its cage to roam around in my head. 'Fuck,' I thought. 'Is he going to change his mind on me again?' Tony F. reassured me during our goalkeeper review but it was still there. It changed the moment a journalist asked me if I was worried Tony G. might opt for another goalkeeper for the next game. Straight away, I said no, I didn't think so. But in my head, I thought, 'No, fuck you. Absolutely not.' Until that very moment, I had been interrogating myself about the same thing but the same thought coming from an external source like that just snapped me out of it and made me want to back myself more. The doubts went away again.

Alanna and I had talked properly about the goal we conceded by then, too. During recovery, we often go to the infrared sauna together. It was just the two of us. One minute, we were sitting in there and everything was normal; the next minute, we were looking at each other and laughing. And we both knew why. One of us said, 'Should we talk about it?' and the other replied, 'Yeah, let's get it off our chest.' Lans said she should have just cleared the ball instead of choosing a backpass. I said I shouldn't have come out of my goal and that I possibly wasn't communicating as well because I tend to go a bit quiet after I make a mistake on the field. We both took accountability and reassured each other that we had both played really well against Ireland – this slip-up wouldn't define us. It was such a good moment. We cleared the air in a really mature way. It was good to know we had it in us. Because we are best mates and not overly serious people around each other, it can be hard to shift the tone to, 'Hey, I think you and me might have fucked up here.'

You never want to fuck up but, in a way, the loss was good for us. It forced us to remember we weren't simply going to sail through the group stage. Where the Ireland win lifted us up, the Nigeria loss brought us crashing back down to earth. The fun was over. We were at a World Cup and shit was getting real. One more loss and it would be all over, red rover. It put us in a very particular mindset heading into what was now a must-win match against Canada.

22.
Game 3, Canada

We knew the calculations. Nigeria needed only to draw with Ireland to qualify for the knockouts. We had to beat Canada. So we put aside the Nigeria vs Ireland bit and just focused on beating Canada. Between our opening two games, we'd had seven full days to let our minds wander and had allowed ourselves to start thinking about the round of 16 already. Who we might be playing and who we might face in the quarter-finals after that. This was dangerous. It's so easy to see how losing touch with the present had made us complacent against Nigeria.

Now we were humbled and only had four days before we were due back on the field. Bev Priestman's Canada are a force – they were reigning Olympic champions for a reason. That said, we knew there were distractions in their camp. The team had spent the six months leading up to the tournament in a dispute with the national federation over pay equity and budget cuts. The squad would have felt drained. They were coming off a 2–1 win over Ireland but had been held to a scoreless draw by Nigeria in their opener. They were beatable. But then they were probably looking at us and thinking the same thing. We had just capitulated to Nigeria. We were rattled. I remember talking about it with Steph, the group's voice of reason. She wasn't worried one bit. She said we play best when our backs are against the wall – that whenever we find ourselves in this position, we come out on top. Steph said this with such conviction that I just believed her immediately. Sweet, I thought. We're going to be fine. Not in an arrogant way or a careless way; I just felt single-minded about it. I could see this attitude had spread around the whole squad, all convinced we were not going to be knocked out.

That sentiment built as we readied to fly to Melbourne on match day minus one, and as we got on the plane and then checked into our hotel at the other end. I blocked out the media. There was some negative chat about us as a team and about me personally that I stopped looking at social media. Punters were saying we needed Sam Kerr; needed to do this and shouldn't have done that. That kind of thing made us mad and I think we partly wanted to play well as a bit of a 'fuck you' to everyone talking shit.

Aussies love an underdog story. We thrive as underdogs – it's our specialty. It helped that Canada were Olympic gold medallists and always do well at major tournaments. Under these circumstances, it didn't take the pressure off us as such but we were so hellbent on proving a point that it didn't matter. I couldn't think about anything else. There was a bit of personal pressure of my own making: the

Matildas hadn't been knocked out in the group stage at a World Cup for 20 years and I didn't want to be the goalkeeper between the sticks when that happened. That feeling didn't manifest as the usual nerves about making a mistake, though; it was more an awareness of the narrative. How would the world react if we exited this early at a home World Cup?

For a few days at least, the night of 31 July was the highlight of my career. The venue was AAMI Park but, because FIFA rules stipulate that sponsorship names must be removed from all official venues, it was renamed Melbourne Rectangular Stadium for the duration of the tournament. Fans on social media quickly translated that to 'MRS', which then became 'The Missus'. And she turned out to be a pretty great place to visit. There are crowds and there are crowds, and this Melbourne lot were next level. The Missus is a boutique ground – a smidge under 28,000 had squeezed in for the game. It was about a third of the number that had piled into Stadium Australia for the Ireland game but the noise in this little place was something else. Supporters had heeded Sam's call two days earlier, when she asked them to do everything in their power to help except for booing during the national anthems. 'The crowd has been absolutely unbelievable,' she said. 'The fans at our hotel, walking down the street, people making us coffee. Like literally everyone has been so supportive and we can feel the love and the girls thrive under that. So, of course, whatever the crowd wants to bring, we're willing to accept that we need them and that's the reason we play.' Ellie had made a point of mentioning it as well. 'You can see over the past two games. The crowd has been massive,' she said. 'Especially against Nigeria in the last 10 minutes; you could feel the crowd and I just knew we were gonna get a goal back in those last 10 minutes. So on Monday, the crowd is so important for us. Having that home crowd, it's massive. It really is going to push us to that final minute.'

At AAMI Park, that translated as chants and cheers, and booing when the video assistant referee ruled a Mary goal offside. Mary did get a goal in the end. Hayley got two and Steph scored another penalty in injury time. After either our third or fourth goal, as we were about to kick off again, I shouted my usual, 'Let's go again, girls.' I'll never forget Alanna turning around and smiling at me. We were so close to laughing. I don't know if we couldn't believe what was happening or if we were just having so much fun. To convert so much pressure into a 4–0 win, we were all so proud of ourselves. Everyone else played outstandingly and the fact we did it once more without Sam was another confidence boost before the knockouts.

TONY FRANKEN

At one point in this game, Macca transferred the ball from one side to the other with a drill that went straight out to Caitlin. Two passes later, we scored. That was textbook from my coaching courses and exactly the type of distribution you can't defend against. She's able to execute that. There are times her distribution can be inconsistent but in general it's very good.

There was a lot of talk around whether Sam might be able to play some part against Canada. The media were going mental with it. She fuelled that fire by volunteering herself for a press conference two days before the game and declaring she was 'definitely going to be available'. But it was happening within camp, as well. We were all like, 'Sam, can you play? Can you come on? How many minutes can you play?' In reality, it would have been very early for her to come back but she was willing to risk it in the Canada match if our World Cup hung on a late goal. We didn't need her to risk it.

Mary and Em were brilliant up front and Cait and Steph were on fire together on the left. It was a big team effort. I didn't end up having all that much to do but I did break my own speed record while running to celebrate Steph's pen. We all followed her to the sideline and jumped in a huddle. As I got up to run back to my goal, Sam grabbed me from the sideline and told me Ireland and Nigeria had drawn 0–0 and that we had topped Group B. That was the first time in days that I had considered anything outside of this match – I had genuinely forgotten about other results. But a photo was taken of Sam and me hugging just after she told me this. It meant we would be playing Denmark instead of England in the round of 16.

Everyone on social media and in the mainstream media seemed to be back on the bandwagon. It also made us realise how fickle the media can be. They had talked shit so easily before this game, and now that we'd put four past the Olympic champions everything was great again. For Alanna and me, our miscommunication against Nigeria had been a big talking point but all that just instantly disappeared. That was when I realised that I needed to block out the media. Not even block it out, really – just not read into it. Had we gone on to lose to Denmark, so many wouldn't have had our backs, so it felt safer to keep it at a distance.

There was one social media presence I definitely did not keep at a distance. Soon after we topped our group, the Brisbane Broncos started following me on Instagram. This was the time the hype started to get noticeably bigger. The coverage wasn't just about Sam anymore but about the rest of us, too. Social media is often the first place people find you and the girls were getting follow notifications from all kinds of celebrities. But my all-time highlight was the Broncos, for sure. My friend Nash, who I went to school with, is an agent for some of the boys who play for Brisbane, like Reece Walsh and a few others. He got a jersey signed for me and brought it to my hotel and I tagged the club's account in a post. Then they started following me. My mind was blown. If you had told me when I was seven or eight years old that the Broncos players would know who I was in 20 years, I would have died on the spot. This was definitely my 'wow – I've made it' moment. I took a screenshot and sent it to my dad and brother, who were beside themselves. I still have that screenshot for safekeeping.

While back in Brisbane, I spent some time with my nieces and we got ready to play Denmark. We moved to a FIFA-sanctioned hotel and said goodbye to our base camp.

Shit was getting real. Brazil, one of our biggest world rivals, had already been knocked out in the group stage. So had Germany. Who would be next? We flew to Sydney on 6 August – match day minus one – and trained that afternoon at the Western Sydney Wanderers' training base, Wanderers Football Park. We completed the first 15 minutes – effectively warm-up drills – in front of all the cameras, which mostly focused on Sam doing slow revolutions on a stationary exercise bike. Once we were alone again, a funny thing happened – a helicopter flew overhead; we later found out it was a News Corp chopper, presumably sent out to glean information on Sam and other tactical bits and pieces. Always ready to make light of every situation, we started sticking our fingers up at it. I think they got one photo of Meeks with her finger up. In Tony's pre-match press conference a couple of hours later, he cracked a hilariously bad joke about the interest in the Matildas going 'sky high'. It was all just noise and we were getting pretty good at being unbothered by it.

That evening was memorable for a couple of reasons. The first was that the United States were knocked out, losing to Sweden on penalties. It was wild to think they were the two-time defending champions, having won in both 2015 and 2019, and had been the best team on the planet for a long time. And suddenly they were out of the picture. Their earliest exit from a World Cup in history. The second was that Kyra Cooney-Cross set off the smoke alarm in our hotel and the firefighters had to come. We basically arrived and all went to shower. We had been advised that once you were in the bathroom, you had to shut the door and stay in there until you were done showering. Kyra either didn't completely shut the door or stepped out for something and it set off all the alarms in the place. The whole thing was very funny because our head of security, Kersten, was stressing out over whether there had been a security breach. She was trying to get us to stay in our rooms, which of course meant we all piled into the hallways, adding to everyone else's panic. The scene was mayhem: Kersten is in the hallway, Kyra is there in a towel, the firies are walking up and down. Eventually, they worked out what had happened and we were allowed to continue settling in for the night. Despite the chaos, we felt relaxed. It was not a feeling I woke up with the following morning.

23.
Round of 16, Denmark

The morning of the match arrived and I couldn't open my eyes. Both were glued shut by a film of pus. I slowly peeled and scraped enough of it off to see, and even then they were very watery and irritated. My bad feeling was confirmed when I looked in the mirror and saw two glassy, pink eyeballs staring back at me. I rang my brother, thinking my nieces must have given me conjunctivitis during one of my visits. It turns out my sister-in-law, Amy, had had it recently. The timing was terrible. I was feeling otherwise fine but knew I must have been highly contagious. I was too afraid to tell any of the coaches because I thought they might tell me I couldn't play or had to stay away from the rest of the team. Amy gave me the name of some eye drops to buy and I caught an Uber down to a nearby Chemist Warehouse. The whole trip took about half an hour but my eyes seemed to get a lot worse during that time. Every time I blinked, my vision got a bit blurry.

In the end, I decided I had to tell our team doctor, Brandi Cole. She came straight to my room to have a look. I told her my eyes felt itchy and sore, as if I had sand in them and couldn't get it out. She gave me some ointment that I had to put into my eye and leave for a bit, then I had to dab my eyes with a warm towel. When I got to the dabbing part of the process, I slipped the towel into my eye and blinked over it. When I pulled it out, there was pus. I think she knew as well as I did what was going on but she kept very calm, even though I was getting pretty stressed. She assured me we would figure it out. I spent the entire day dabbing my eye with the towel to try and get the pus out. I didn't like the feeling of it but I could deal with it if it meant my vision would clear up. Blurry vision as a goalkeeper is not ideal, as you can imagine. But this was the situation. If I wanted to play our first World Cup knockout match, I just had to get on with it.

At Stadium Australia, as I was running back down the tunnel after our warm-up, my brother was standing there. He asked me how my eyes were. Without thinking, I said, 'They're fucked,' and then kept running. I felt guilty when I got back into the changeroom. Sam and Dad had flown down just for the game and I was concerned they would spend the whole match worrying about it. I texted him to say they were actually fine and not to stress about it.

LYDIA WILLIAMS

Before a match, straight after you have the team photo and talk in the huddle and are about to run to your position on the field, one of the back-up goalkeepers gives the starting goalkeeper their water bottle and towel, and a little high five with a good luck. I knew something was up with Mac's eyes because she asked me to prepare two towels – one wet and one dry. Then I saw her squeezing her eyes and was like, 'Ew, that's coming from your face?' She told me she could hardly see. So I had her towels ready and passed them over just before kick-off, thinking, 'Yuck. Here you go.'

Nobody else from within the team had said anything to me so I could only assume Brandi had kept quiet. She put in some eye drops just as I was about to walk out for kick-off and that helped for about 15 minutes. After that, I was on my own. During every little break in play, I would try to quickly grab the towel and wipe my eyes. We got one such break after 20 minutes, when, under significant pressure from Pernille Harder, Steph had what she described as 'a little roll' of her ankle, which required a stoppage in play while she was checked out by medical staff. While that was happening, the rest of us huddled near the bench. The short break allowed us to recalibrate and we took complete control after that. Steph turned out to be just fine and later called her injury a 'happy coincidence'.

We won 2–0 and it felt great. The Canada game was backs against the wall; this felt like a professional win. In the 29th minute, Mary let fly with that perfect through ball, Cait outran defender Stine Ballisager Pedersen, and nutmegged Denmark's goalkeeper Lene Christensen. Then, in the 70th, Hayley scored her third goal of the tournament. Sam even got subbed on for 15 minutes at the end, getting the loudest cheer.

After it was over, Tony F. approached me. 'Uh-oh,' I thought. 'I might be in trouble here.' I stood in front of him, wiping my eyes like a maniac, waiting to hear what he had to say. He praised me for getting through another game and said the fact I had done so with conjunctivitis was further proof of my improved mentality. He had obviously found out at some stage. When I saw Brandi afterwards for treatment, she said Tony F. had had a little mid-match freakout from our bench and asked her to do something to help me – I clearly had something stuck in my eyes. She apparently told him then and said I was trying to get through it the best I could. After the game, I admitted to my brother that my eyes had actually felt pretty bad.

I tried to head straight down the tunnel to our changeroom but a FIFA official blocked the door and told me I had to walk through the mixed zone. The mixed zone is a cordoned-off section inside the stadium where broadcast and print media conduct interviews with players. Players aren't obliged to stop and give interviews but it is compulsory to at least walk through. All I could think about was getting into the shower and rubbing my eyes, and this guy was trying to get me to do media. Aside from being infectious, it felt like an embarrassing, gross type of illness to tell media about. So I looked at FIFA man and said, 'Mate, unless you want the whole mixed zone to catch conjunctivitis,

I suggest you get out of my way.' He took one look at my eyes and let me pass through, no further questions asked.

The infection got worse overnight and the following morning my eyelids were pasted shut even more than they had been the day before. Throughout recovery and the next few days of training, I stayed away from the girls as much as I could. I was hammering my eyes with that ointment – anything to make me stop wanting to scratch my eyeballs out. They slowly cleared up and everything in camp began to feel calm.

I stayed in my room a lot during this period for obvious reasons. Under normal circumstances, I would get FOMO if I knew the girls were hanging out and I wasn't there. I'm very social and find it hard to say no if something is happening. Luckily for me, there wasn't a proper common room at this hotel, which meant fewer FOMO opportunities. And taking that out of the equation allowed me to focus only on myself and getting mentally and physically ready for the Saturday at Suncorp Stadium. As a team, we were starting to feel unstoppable. We had beaten France only a few weeks earlier and knew we could do it again. But we weren't too complacent, in the way we may have been against Nigeria. France's manager, Hervé Renard, had successfully rehabilitated the national team in the five months since he was appointed during a period of unprecedented crisis. The France Football Federation had sacked former manager Corinne Diacre after captain Wendie Renard and teammates Marie-Antoinette Katoto and Kadidiatou Diani announced they would boycott the national team if the current set-up remained. So Hervé, who had just led the Saudi Arabian men's side to an upset group-stage defeat of Lionel Messi's eventual champions Argentina at the 2022 World Cup, left that job and joined France's women. They had started slow at this tournament, with a scoreless draw against Jamaica, but grown into their campaign with a 2–1 win over Brazil and a 6–3 thrashing of Panama to top Group F. Then they did a 4–0 number on Morocco in the round of 16.

I awoke on the Friday, 11 August, with more pus seeping out the corners of my eyes. The doctor said I had stopped antibiotics too early and directed me to restart them. Twenty-four hours later, on game day, my eyes were still not completely better but a hell of a lot closer to it than on the day of the Denmark game. And if I could play under those circumstances, I could definitely deal with this. Plus I had a win on the superstition front that settled all of our nerves. The girls had been asking me what colour kit I'd been assigned for the quarter-final. I found out on 12 August I would be wearing the black strip. When I told a few teammates, it was almost funny how pumped they were. This small, inconsequential detail spread like wildfire through the squad and became this good omen heading into the game. I don't think any of us really believed it meant anything and, to be honest, I've never been overly superstitious. We just knew I had worn black for the Ireland opener and we were pretty fired up that night in Sydney – and I could do with a bit more of that energy.

24.

Quarter-final, France

'The crowd sounds really loud tonight,' I thought as I walked up the tunnel and out onto the field for the warm-up. It's not as if they hadn't made noise at our previous games but this felt different, as if I had surround sound switched on in high definition. Queensland State of Origin fans didn't call this place The Cauldron for nothing. I headed to the goal and started our regular drills with Tony F., Lyds and Teagan. Suncorp Stadium wasn't even close to full yet – but still the cheers were pretty damn loud. For two or three minutes, I was pretty pleased that everyone was so enthusiastic to see three goalkeepers serving up balls to each other. Then I realised I'd forgotten to take my hearing aids out. Of course. I removed them and the volume in the theatre room turned back down.

It was the first time I'd accidentally walked out for a game with the devices still in my ears. I wasn't put off by it, though. I wasn't put off by anything at this stage. I felt unshakeable. Athletes can spend their entire careers chasing the elusive state they call 'the zone'. Some achieve it many times; others only a few or never at all. Modern sports psychologists offer techniques to assist an athlete hoping to enter this optimal space at will so they can find 'flow': the perfect match between an activity's perceived demands and the person's abilities. A complete absorption in the task at hand, to the point that the person's sense of time is transformed. It began to happen from the moment we were lined up in the tunnel and heard Uncle Shannon Ruska delivering the Welcome to Country – in this case, a First Nations-language version of 'Waltzing Matilda' to the sounds of didgeridoo under the darkening Brisbane sky. 'It's just like how Europe has France, Italy, Germany. When we go to those borders, we always yell out and seek permission,' Uncle Shannon said. 'One way is by singing in language. And now, the didgeridoo player here tonight, he is one of my in-laws. My wife is from a little town in Central Queensland called Winton. There was actually a famous song that comes from that area. It's the local tribe from that area, it's the local tribe from there. In fact, Banjo Paterson made the song. I will sing it now, in Aboriginal. Then I will get you to join in on the chorus.' Hearing him sing, and then the crowd joining in, gave me goosebumps. We stood there, about to play in front of a nation with a culture more enduring than a 29-year-old like me could comprehend. France, in blue, lined up next to us so close I could have literally reached out and grabbed one of their hands. But I didn't – I just kept chewing my caffeine gum. Nobody from either team even glanced at the other. All eyes were right ahead, looking out towards the light, towards the unknown. Then, with Steph directly in front of me and Cait directly behind, we walked out to the dramatic rendition of 'Seven Nation Army' played at this stage before every World Cup fixture. After that came the actual anthems of each nation. Alongside the Australian flag also hung the Aboriginal and Torres Strait Islander flags. Underneath these symbols of unity, we sang, arm in arm and with glassy eyes (my pink eyes especially).

Then, it is time. With my gloves already on, I strip off my jacket to reveal the black kit underneath. We pose for our team photo and I jog off towards our designated goal. The keeper up the other end is Pauline Peyraud-Magnin, the Juventus and France first choice. She made her international debut several years after me but has significantly more caps. This would have meant more to me a year ago. Right now, it does not even register. Beyond these 7000-odd square metres of perfectly preened grass is the most potent home support. People from where I grew up playing. People I probably passed in the car on the way to training in the QAS days, on the street while playing for Brisbane Roar. People who might have sat next to me in the stands at this very stadium. Maybe the man who copped splashes of my Fanta all over his jacket is up there somewhere. And if they aren't here, those people might be watching on TV. People who didn't know or care who we were before last month – perhaps even before last week. Aidan was right – this is the moment I needed to work towards. The one I would have regretted watching from the bench. The one that is starting right now.

France is on the attack, again and again, until their left-back Sakina Karchaoui puts in a cross and I gather. Then Alanna tugs on the shirt of Kadidiatou Diani and the striker shoots just wide of my far post. And France have all the early corners. One finds Maëlle Lakrar, only for the centre-back to miscue her first shot under pressure. Those two early scares settle the contest but France spend the first 40 minutes winning the pressing battle. I dive to my right and hit the ground hard with arms still outstretched, vetoing Eugénie Le Sommer – France's first shot on target. Clare Hunt clears a shot from Kenza Dali. I punch away another corner and turn the follow-up shot around my near post in the nick of time. After all of this, in the 41st minute, Ellie runs away from me, down the right, and Hayley cuts back to Em, and Em lays off to Mary. She knows exactly what to do with an open goal but De Almeida knows exactly how to get her body in the way for a goal-line clearance that denies us a lead before half-time.

In the second half, we start the better team. Sam is warming up after five minutes and on the field after 10 – the high-definition surround sound has been switched back on, even though my hearing aids are definitely not in this time. With Sam comes momentum. In the 79th minute, she finds open space where there is none and releases a pass with Hayley in mind but our winger isn't there yet.

And then, in the 90th, Selma Bacha takes a long-range shot that is always drifting wide. Three minutes of stoppage time later, referee María Carvajal blows her whistle to signal the end of regular time. We have had the better of the second half but no goal to show for it. But we have kept France out, too.

We retreat to our technical area to suck down gels and chew on lollies. The French are swallowing some kind of purée in theirs. After a few minutes of downtime, we are back on the field and into the first 15 minutes of extra time.

The rhythm is similar, if a little fatigued. But the 50,000 watching are still full of energy and ready to boo when France are awarded a corner, even though the ball last touched French substitute Vicki Bècho before bobbling over the byline and out of play. The corner finds Alanna, who heads the ball down – but it's tracking for the space to my left when the momentum of my body is already moving to my right. And then it's in the net – we've scored an own goal before I can even blink. When I open my eyes, Lans is on her stomach on the turf, face contorted into the shock of conceding the goal that might well end our tournament. I blink again and Carvajal is disallowing the goal. I help Lans up as the VAR shows Wendie Renard tugging Cait down as she contests the header. Renard is beside herself. We all are.

Where regular-time momentum was cordoned off neatly into halves, extra time is constant changes in possession and half-chances – except for Cortnee Vine, who has a full chance. I take a goal kick that finds Sam's head and then

Mini's and then Cait. She is onside and crosses for Cortnee. And while our substitute's run to the near post is flawless, she cannot quite negotiate the acute angle. A minute later, I gather a loose ball and we take our leave to prepare for the second half of extra time.

This next part is all a blur. I know I am physically there in the 107th minute, when Bècho winds up for a shot at the edge of the box and our entire backline stick out various limbs to try and thwart it. My reaction to the bullet rushing my way is to propel my body skyward in a spring and leap to my right, then to stick up a left glove to cover the remaining distance. I get there, parry the ball away and jump to my feet, yelling, 'Come on – let's go!' I know that I am there as France rain down on us with everything they've got. I see Grace Geyoro cross and Alanna collide with Le Sommer. I deny Bècho in second-half injury time as Solène Durand is brought on to replace Peyraud-Magnin in goal. But it is all a blur because the thought of penalties is inching its way forward from the back of my mind until it's all I can think about.

SHAQUILLE BOND

I was sitting next to Sam and his wife, Amy, and they had their girls on their laps. Leah and Steve were there, too. We were just sitting there praying it wouldn't go to penalties. We all knew her career so well and what it had been like not being the starter for so long and not getting to play big games. And we just couldn't stop thinking that penalties could mean the whole country was either going to love her or potentially hate her.

I desperately want the thought of penalties to disappear until I have no choice but to confront it, but I know that won't happen until I hear the final whistle. When that sounds, a penalty shootout is confirmed and Tony G. is looking at me with those five fingers in the air.

TONY FRANKEN

I don't think Mackenzie was expecting that. She does take quite a good penalty kick, so through all the practice we did, she was quite high up in the order. Then, with the substitutions we had made, she was elevated further. I think that threw her a little bit, learning she was actually going to take a penalty and having to deal with the enormity of that situation. Because when I was talking to her about the various French kickers, she said, 'Tony, I'll look to you for the signal.' I took that to mean: 'I don't want information now. I've got enough to think about. I'll look at you for every penalty.' In that situation, there is no use trying to overload her with specifics, so I simply said, 'No worries. All the best.' As it turned out, she faced 10 penalty takers and she would've lost a lot of the information anyway.

Macca doesn't like writing her own instructions on a water bottle or a towel as some keepers do. She prefers to take her information in as it comes. We were all comfortable with that. If she looked up at me, I would give her the information we had discussed – then it was up to her as to what she did with that information.

The way we collect intel these days is so different, too. Going back to 2005, when the Socceroos were preparing for possible penalties in our 2006 World Cup qualifying play-off against Uruguay, it was the days of DVDs and CDs, and there wasn't nearly as much recorded footage. Information gathering was largely anecdotal, in that it more came down to people like John Aloisi saying, 'Richard Morales played with me at Osasuna and he usually does this.' That has changed hugely in both the men's and women's games. The Matildas' video analysts go through hundreds of international and club games featuring the opponents' players, over about a two-year period, and send me a PowerPoint or something similar with all the information synthesised. I then look at the footage and come up with what I think might happen with each player. After that, we do the same thing as a group. I ask them for their thoughts without telling them what I'm thinking. Generally, we all come to the same conclusion.

Anyway, we'd practised what I wanted her to do and I was showing her evidence of her making saves. She used the technique we'd practised and saved France's fifth penalty – the one from Ève Périsset that was heading for the corner. Had she used her own technique for that one, I don't know if she would've got it. But I would also never chastise a goalkeeper for doing something different to what I instructed because I'm not the one playing in front of 50,000 people. And Mackenzie also made a couple of saves using her routine, so who am I to say it was wrong to do that? Mackenzie's focus was there and I had full trust in her to do what she believed best each time. Shootouts are not a team activity – they're individual. It's a keeper versus a striker. The keeper is given the intel and then they go with their gut. And it was with her gut that she decided she wanted to do her routine for some of the kicks.

CAITLIN FOORD

I'm glad I advised Macca to stick to her strengths, because I could see during that training session she was frustrated the new way wasn't working for her. If I'm good at something on the pitch and I was told to change that, why would I do that? That's what I'm good at. It just didn't make sense to me.

LYDIA WILLIAMS

I was just doing whatever I could to help in that moment. I knew I wasn't going to be playing. That was something Tony and I spoke about for a long time, so we had penalty-shootout video sessions, going over what we would both be doing during it. I was with Franken on the bench as he gave her the signals. Everyone else was gathered on the field and we were doing signals of each person we had, which way they would go or what we thought. Because I actually had a job to do during the shootouts, I wasn't too wrapped up in the emotions. Knowing Mac from a really young age, she's always been pretty exceptional at penalties and kicking. They are things I really admired about her growing up. She has a unique knack. And watching as she trained and prepared for this possibility, I felt quietly confident in her ability.

After I miss my penalty, the score stands at 3–3 after five spot kicks each. I have saved two – one with my technique and one with the one Tony F. taught me. I had decided to use both, depending on the identity of the kicker, the signal delivered by Tony F. and my own intuition. The obvious question here is: after missing my kick, does my confidence to pull off either turn to shit?

STEVE ARNOLD

I thought, 'What the hell is she doing having a shot?' Then I thought 'Well, if she gets this, it'll be a fairytale.' But, of course, she missed that. And when she missed, I did think that could well be the end of it.

I guess I would say that, if it is possible to measure time in tiny moments, then there are probably a few milliseconds of mental decay directly after it clattered into the upright. But then two things happen in quick succession. Behind me, I hear the voice of one of the girls yell, 'You got this, Mac!' And in front of me, Tony F. simply lifts his hands in my direction – resurrecting me without words. It is honestly all I need. Yes, it is deflating not to have won it for us but we are still very much in this and I have a central role to play.

DARREN LOCKYER, rugby league legend

Our family watched that quarter-final together at home. I had heard the name Mackenzie Arnold before but I'd never really watched a game that intensely. That penalty shootout was pretty captivating. She just always looked confident within herself. Not for one moment did I feel she was losing her ability to focus. I know from experience that when you're out in the middle and there are a lot of people watching – for us league players, it's during Origin – you're not really thinking about the crowd or the people watching on TV. You have a really narrow focus on what you need to do. So for her to miss that kick and then get back in goal and put that behind her was a testament to her character. Just to let go of what happened, say, 'What's done is done,' and move on. Had she dwelled on the mistake, she wouldn't have executed what she did next.

Because both teams have now taken five penalties and the score is tied at 3–3, the shootout will go to sudden death. If France convert the next kick and we then miss ours, we lose. If France miss and then we convert, we win. If both teams either convert or miss, penalties continue until option A or B occurs.

Geyoro takes a bit of time to get to the spot for her kick. It gives me a chance to gather my thoughts and bring myself fully back to the present. She outwits me with a stalled run-up. Even though I get a palm onto the ball, she scores. She stops almost dead still before taking her shot and I am straight over to the referee to protest. A kicker must be moving in a forward motion at all times and I believe this stretches the rule to the point of maybe breaking it. The referee disagrees. Though I'm peeved about it, the events of the past 30 seconds have well and truly moved me on from my missed penalty. Between my misconstrued wind-up and Geyoro's moment of gamesmanship, I'm back in the present. I pick up the ball and walk over to our next penalty taker. Mini takes the ball with steely focus and walks to the spot. She has to score to keep us in it. When she does, she wheels off and celebrates with a rocking baby motion – a reference to Harper, her daughter – and kisses the tape on her wrist, which has a message for her partner Clara. Clara's father passed away in the lead-up to this game.

KIRSTY SMITH

I was so furious because we had a friendly at exactly the same time as the game. So I was watching the game in the changeroom and it probably would've finished just before we started, but then it went to extra time. It was extra time and I still had it on my phone in the changeroom, and then it obviously went to penalties. I just couldn't miss out on what was going to happen, so I got the kit woman for the game to literally watch the game at the side of the pitch while I was warming up to keep me updated on whether they'd scored or if it had been saved. Every two minutes she would say, 'Yes, she scored.' Some of the other girls were quite invested in it, too, so we'd be cheering. And then she told us that Mac had been up to take a penalty and I thought, 'Oh my God, please score.' When I was told she had missed, I just hoped to God my game didn't start before the penalty shootout had finished. Because it would have put me off my game. I was on an emotional rollercoaster in a warm-up!

We are at the point where Tony F. no longer has much analysis to work with. This is already a longer shootout than most and I know the next few will be on me to figure out. Karchaoui hits the roof of the net and I dive the right way but miss by a couple of centimetres. This gives me confidence. I have so much faith in the girls to keep scoring. All they need is for me to save one and give them the chance to finish the job. Meeks puts hers past Durand. Then Lakrar scores against me and that pisses me off. I start to feel myself losing some of the technical elements of my technique. I am going too early and giving up my game plan before my opponent has kicked it.

> **SHAQUILLE BOND**
>
> Leah had to leave mid-penalty shootout because it was too much. She couldn't watch, so she literally went to the bathroom. Amy, Sam and I were squeezing each other so tight. It was just one of the most intense experiences.

This has already been going an age. We are into a third hour – a rarity in football. I don't yet know if I am tired either, because the adrenaline is like nothing else. I keep refocusing. Keep telling myself we have practised this and I need to have faith. And when Ellie slots her penalty in off the post and celebrates in the way only Ellie can, I think, 'Nah, this is it now.' I think that once more as I see who France's next kicker is. Kenza Dali is an ex-teammate at West Ham. I know I've got her even before her body language betrays any tangible signs. I know she is a technical player and I know she will open up. I don't know why or how I know and I don't think consciously about my decision to dive instinctively to my left and palm the ball around the post.

> **DARREN LOCKYER**
>
> I live close enough to Suncorp to hear the crowd – probably less than a kilometre away. And because TV broadcasts operate on a slight delay, we can normally tell from our couch whether or not a goal has been scored a couple of seconds before we see it on our screen.

If anyone was ever going to accuse me of being cocky, this moment would be it. I've never celebrated so hard in my life. I turn around to the team and roar. It feels like a big 'fuck you' to everything that has happened before. I'm so wrapped up in it that it takes me a while to see what everyone else has already seen. Surely not. This cannot be happening. The referee is signalling a retake because I have come off my line. I watch the VAR replay on the big screen and my foot has indeed left the goal line early.

So back I go to face Kenza again. We are 18 kicks into this shootout and it is already the longest in World Cup history. Before I even get there, I've decided I will dive the same way. Kenza has a stubborn personality and I know she will want to prove a point. She lines up the same. And sure enough, she hits it the same. A little sweeter than before but this time I'm already halfway there. I have denied her twice. To avoid the potential embarrassment of another mid-celebration letdown, I stay on my knees and stare out the ref until she confirms that I have not reoffended. Then I rise to my feet, turn around and lift my hands up to the crowd. The noise in reply is like nothing I have ever heard before. The feeling is blood-pumping, spine-tingling elation. My appreciation falls to this mass of people who have bought tickets to be here and then carried me through this 17-minute marathon. I owe it all to them.

BRUCE KAIDER

Aidan sent me a really nice text message that basically said, 'Fuck, mate. We both knew this would happen. We believed in it.' And I replied, 'We did, man.' I said, 'I hope you are enjoying a moment here seeing this, because you have truly been one of her biggest supporters, even when there were probably others who weren't supporting her.' I couldn't be more proud of what she's achieved. And it wasn't gifted to her – she did the work. She was ready for that moment.

As it turns out, the penalty shootout is *still* not over. Durand saves Clare Hunt's spot kick but, even then, I know France can no longer stem the bleeding. Bècho hits the post and Cortnee steps up for the chance to take it all.

Viney is one of those players who has no idea how good she really is. Before this World Cup – her first – she spoke publicly about imposter syndrome and waiting for everyone to figure out she was a fraud. Strangely, that mental space has pushed her to incredible breakthroughs over the past couple of years. This next one will live with her forever.

MARK SCHWARZER, Socceroos legend

I came away from that night in disbelief at what I had just witnessed. Yes, I've experienced shootouts before in huge games, including a quite well-known one against Uruguay in 2005. But this was something else and will, in my opinion, go down as the biggest performance of any Australian goalkeeper.

As soon as Viney steps up, I know the game is over. She slots it home and the celebrations begin. I've never run so fast as I did to get over to the girls. There were screams, tears, hugs, laughs, everything in between. I don't think any of us will ever be able to put the emotions from that moment into words. It's crazy to look back now and realise that our lives had just changed forever.

Part of our job this World Cup is to inspire the next generation and hearing how many people are watching our games, coming to our games, having live sites around Australia – they're showing our game in four major stadiums – that's just incredible. When we rock up to the games and see everyone in our jerseys and screaming fans, it's touching and, honestly, it makes me a bit emotional because it's just so amazing. This is what we wanted to do. We wanted to inspire the next generation and pave the way for women's football in Australia.

I made sure I shook hands with the French players I passed and congratulated them on their tournament. When I ran into Tony G., he was bawling and gave me the biggest hug. I thanked him for believing in me. He told me he always believed in me. Then I had to find Tony Franken, the person I felt I owed this whole moment too. We were both teary-eyed at that point, and I'll never forget sharing that experience with him. He was the reason I was where I was. All the hard work that he had put in for me behind the scenes had just come to fruition – everything I had gone through, he had been the one to talk me through it. The tears, the shitty days and everything in between – all of a sudden it made sense.

TONY FRANKEN

I didn't sleep for two days afterwards. I didn't think it was affecting me that much but it obviously did. I was still so wound up and, with the adrenaline still going through the body, I just couldn't sleep. It was just the body coming down from a high, I reckon. It took me two days to actually get back to normal again.

Lastly, I found my family. My dad and my brother were both crying, a sight I never thought I'd ever see. Mum had left and returned to her seat three times because she couldn't watch. I hugged them all tight. I have wanted to make them proud for so long. Maybe they were proud already but this was when I felt as if I had finally done it.

SHAQUILLE BOND

I rushed to the front of the stands and bunched up with everyone else against the railing near the tunnel. Then I saw Kenz and we made eye contact. As she ran over, I dropped my arm down and she jumped up for a high five. Then we were just laughing and yelling at each other, letting out, 'Oh my god', at the top of our lungs. She could only stay for a minute before having to head back and continue on the victory lap. People around me who'd been watching kept asking me how I know her and telling me I'm so lucky. 'Oh my god,' they said. 'I can't believe she high fived you.' It's just crazy that people were so invested. And it is just so funny to me because before this, soccer (especially women's soccer) was not a big sport in Australia at all, but the whole stadium – and country, for that matter – was in complete hysteria. It was honestly one of the most stressful, surreal and best moments of my life.

I was named player of the match, which meant I attended the post-match press conference. A reporter commented that my eyes appeared glassy and asked if this win had made me emotional. I was too embarrassed to reveal I had conjunctivitis, so simply said, 'I haven't been too well in the last couple of weeks.'

25.
Afterglow

The morning after the win over France, I awoke to a text message from a friend. It was a photo of a big Nike billboard in Queen Street Mall. The person on it was me. I am wearing my purple kit, so I think the image must be from the Canada game. I texted my contact at Nike and said, 'Thank you so much – this is so cool.' He told me he had commissioned it the night before and their team didn't stop, to make sure it would be there when Brisbane hit the shops on Sunday morning. It was so sick. And I had only just signed with Nike. Before that, I was with Puma, on a deal originally struck by the agent I had before BK. The latest iteration of the contract had run out at the beginning of 2023 and Puma terminated its agreement with me. They said they would not renew because I did not play for a 'top-tier club'. I wasn't even playing for the Matildas at the time. Puma agreed to still provide me with boots and gloves but I told BK that Nike had always been my dream. If boots and gloves would be the extent of it, I would rather receive those items from Nike.

Nike initially told us that goalkeeper jerseys were not a part of the bigger picture and the talks went back and forth for a few months. During this time, I had my Cup of Nations breakthrough and won player of the tournament. We revisited with Puma. Again, they said no. Nike finally came to the party after I represented the Matildas against England and Scotland, when it looked more likely I would start in the World Cup. A contract was agreed just before the tournament and, suffice to say, I would have got a far sweeter deal had I waited another three weeks. But I don't regret it for a minute. All I had ever wanted was to sign with Nike and it is so cool to know I'm with them – they gave me a chance when it seemed no one else would. And now they had erected this billboard for me in a mall where I spent time growing up.

The day only got more surreal from there. My phone had been blowing up all night and there were just too many messages to read, let alone respond to. I did reply to the ones from my friends and people from school and football. But I didn't read any articles or anything on social media. It was all really overwhelming. I did post a series of photos from the night on Instagram and the comments went crazy. I actually recorded the sound of all the notifications coming through on my phone and sent it to Shaquille. The pings were so close together that they formed almost one rhythm of sound for half an hour straight. Mum sent me a photo of the *Courier Mail* – there was a picture of me on the front page with the headline 'There Goes Our Hero'. And the *Gold Coast Bulletin* ran with 'Our Saving Ace'. It was all ridiculous in my mind. Yeah, okay, we just won a penalty shootout. But there goes our hero? Fuck me, relax. So dramatic. Obviously I'm kidding here, but the whole thing was just funny to me.

But some of the other little things were so cool. My primary school, for example, put a notification out for students to wear green and gold on a day that week to celebrate the success of past student Mackenzie Arnold. And then there were streets temporarily named after us – Arnold Court and Caitlin Foord Avenue. It felt like our team was taking over a bit. We loved the videos so much. The ones of AFL crowds leaving their seats to watch our match on the concourse. And the video of all those people on a plane watching the shootout on their little in-flight screens – every single person on the flight, except for that guy watching *The Lord of the Rings*. It cracked me up.

Before we flew to Sydney to prepare for our semi-final against England, I had breakfast with my whole family. We ate at the hotel my parents were staying at. It was pretty early – there weren't even cameras outside our hotel at this stage – and we assumed it would be pretty quiet. But when we went upstairs to eat, all of these heads turned. I felt so self-conscious, wondering what they were all looking at. We sat down at a table and I started playing with my nieces, trying not to acknowledge any of the eyes watching. Then a mother and daughter behind me asked if we could have a photo together and offered their congratulations on the World Cup. I said thanks and it was really nice. But then all these other people saw the interaction and started to make their way over to our table. Before we knew it, half the place was lined up for a photo and the breakfast had turned into a meet and greet. My parents were looking at me and I was looking at them, and we were all thinking, 'What is happening?' It was the first time anything like that had happened to me. Before the World Cup, I didn't have any fan interactions to speak of, though I observed these interactions frequently because I was often hanging out with the main starters. But whenever we were stopped in the street, I usually just kept walking – nine times out of 10, they weren't asking for a photo of me. Sometimes, the girls would include me by telling me that a given person wanted me in the photo, too. I didn't mind not being in the spotlight then but I was even more grateful for it on this particular morning. After a lot of mingling, however, it got to the point where I was close to having to leave my family again – and I wanted to actually sit down and have breakfast with them. I started to think, 'Is this what it's like for people like Sam when they go out?' It was a surreal moment that caught me by surprise.

When we left our hotel to head to the airport, there were cameras *everywhere*. People had gathered around and were asking for photos and autographs. But nothing matched the euphoria of the bus ride to the airport. The vibe was just so high. All the girls were talking about different things that had happened overnight and who had contacted them and what they'd seen. Usually, the bus is a pretty quiet space but today everyone was on their phones showing each other photos and memes and relaying stories and memories from the night before. To put it simply, we were all just really happy. I felt on top of the world. The usual feeling that stays with me for 24 hours after I've played well was multiplied by about 10. I felt weightless. We had just made the final four of a World Cup and taken the entire country with us. Everything had fallen into place for the team at the same time as it had fallen into place for me. I used to picture myself winning a penalty shootout at a major tournament, before even playing at a major tournament had become a realistic possibility (I used to think about scoring a winning penalty, too, but we know how that went). I don't know why I thought about that but it used to replay in my head over and over. Now the biggest event that could have possibly happened did happen. I had just saved three penalties in a penalty shootout.

But there was another layer to it all, one of belonging. I was a real, valued member of this team now. My teammates, who have always said they needed me off the field, now needed me on it. And I was no longer invisible to the outside world, getting off the bus and slipping past fans and media unnoticed. I had received next to no media requests before the World Cup started and next to no approaches from Matildas fans in the street. Now I couldn't even board a bus without being mobbed.

The airport was mad. Again, there were cameras everywhere. Qantas staff had always set up a walkway for us,

standing in a line with yellow and green balloons and clap-
ping us through. They were there again but all the other
people and yet more cameras was a new experience. Fans
were screaming our names and trying to get our autographs
and security were telling them to back away. Real bouncer
shit. We waited for the plane in a private seating area at
the gate. Other people weren't allowed in but it also wasn't
really gated. A couple of girls stood right at the entrance
and kept yelling my name. That was the first time anybody
had specifically selected me from the team for an auto-
graph. Of course, I wasn't their only target but there was
novelty in the fact I was a target at all.

As Australians who largely live and play overseas, we are
used to flying a lot. But I can't even count how many interstate flights we boarded during the World Cup. Many of the
planes we flew on were just for us. That meant a few business seats at the front, reserved for the most capped Matildas
and a row for each of the rest of us behind.

When we arrived in Sydney, the scene was similar to
Brisbane. We are pretty low key compared to some other
national teams – when I say this, I am thinking of the
US. Some of their players get dressed up to travel and
they know where the cameras are. We're happy to pose
for photos and sign autographs but we don't drive it ourselves. Which is why, when we had some stiff competition
at Sydney Airport, it was more of a curiosity than anything
else. At the exact same time as we were exiting the airport,
a guy was getting arrested not far from us. We were all trying to work out what this gentleman had done to be put in

handcuffs and some of the TV crews seemed to be trying to decide who they were there for – him or us. And because we were all within the vicinity of each other, some were trying to do both. There were cameras outside our hotel, too. They would literally film us leaving the hotel and then returning. We would laugh about it, because we couldn't work out what they got out of it. Like, what were they actually filming? We were doing nothing.

My only actual issue came when the TV reporters asked dumb questions. After the France game, I was asked: 'How did you sleep?' I can't fathom why that is useful information for him to know. It's not as if I'm going to turn around and say, 'Actually, I slept fucking terribly. Do you have any tips?'

All of this media stuff was small fry compared with the challenge fast approaching. Facing England at Stadium Australia would be our biggest game yet – we were playing for a place in the final and having to do it against the European champions. Living in the UK, I knew all about the hype around the Lionesses. And it is warranted. They are a superb team who, at the time of our match, were world no. 4. We were world no. 10. We knew how organised they were under manager Sarina Wiegman. But we also knew what we had just done ourselves. No World Cup host nation since the United States in 2003 had reached the final four and here we were, via the most dramatic route you can think of. We had also beaten England in April. Though the circumstances of that 2–0 friendly were vastly different, confidence is confidence no matter how you spin it.

Add that the draw had opened up for us. The world's top two, in Germany (no. 2) and the US (no. 1) went out in the group stage and round of 16 respectively. Brazil (no. 8) also did not make it out of their group. We knocked out Canada (no. 7), then removed Denmark (no. 13) and France (no. 5). Then Spain (no. 6) got rid of the Netherlands (no. 9).

The other three remaining teams were teams we had beaten within the past nine months. Sweden (no. 3) and Spain were set to play the other semi-final in Auckland the night before our massive game in Sydney. Throughout the campaign, Tony G. had only changed his starting line-up when he absolutely had to. Necessity came into play once again when it became clear that Alanna had sustained a concussion during the head clash with Le Sommer. She had been up and down in the couple of days since the game. Then she joined in at training but felt sick that night. There was a lot of discussion with the doctor and the rest of us didn't really know what was going on until she was officially ruled out of our semi-final.

It was obviously a big blow for Lans, who had come back from a couple of injuries to be fit and in form just in time for the tournament. She had started all five of our games alongside Clare Hunt, so this verdict from doctors would have been tough. It was also hard for the rest of us to be there for her in a meaningful way because we were trying to stay positive and not be brought down too much.

It's always a fine balance and one I have certainly experienced from the other side.

It was the morning of the game when we were told. We had a team walk and Lans didn't come. Then we were pulled into a meeting room and Tony G. let us know she had been ruled out and that Polks would step in. I felt torn because Alanna is my best mate but we were also just so thrilled that Polks – our most-capped player ever – would have a chance to start a match at her fifth World Cup. This might realistically have been her last World Cup so it was a nice moment to share with her.

I experienced another first during these few days, when I joined Tony G. for the official pre-match press conference. Typically, one player takes on this task. It can fall to the captain, as was the case with Sam before the Ireland game; then there was Steph before Nigeria, Em before Canada, Cait before Denmark and Ellie before France. Now me before England. I think Steph might have been down to do it because Sam couldn't. And then, well, Steph couldn't either. So our media manager, Ann Odong, came to me. I was a little freaked out – I had never done one before. Ann assured me that it was totally fine if I didn't want to do it. I ended up speaking to Sam about it. She had seen it on the schedule and said something like, 'Oh, a big press conference,' to which I replied that I was actually a bit nervous. She let me know in a very low-key way that I would be fine. My level of stress over it wasn't crushing; I just struggle with any interview that is live because I fear saying the wrong thing. If I am talking about myself,

I am all right, because I'm across all the facts. It's when I get asked about a topic not within my remit or expertise that I flounder. Sam had previously relayed stories about getting hit with curly questions around Indigenous rights or sexuality. But she predicted that, given they were more 'live' issues pre-tournament, and that I had just played a pivotal role in our quarter-final win and might have to do the same against England, it was unlikely I would be asked about much of anything not directly involving our campaign. If I was, there were ways around giving direct answers, such as conceding I am not as educated as I would like to be on a topic and I would like to get better. Sam and Steph gave me a few little tips like that.

Tony G. and I sat down with Ann for our briefing before the press conference. It mainly focused on using words, phrases and ideas that would put the pressure back on England rather than us. The idea was to cultivate a narrative that we were the underdogs and draw attention away from the fact we had beaten the Lionesses only recently and had also beaten Team GB at the most recent Olympics. I wouldn't say we were favourites by any stretch but Tony G. wanted to remove the notion of an even playing field. So he went into that press conference and waxed lyrical about how talented England's players were and the superiority of their resources and youth-development pathways. The message for me was to play down our rivalry with England, because there would be a lot of British journalists who would attempt to elicit a line from me about how huge it was. They had already been hitting a couple of

England's players up with this sort of leading line of questioning, asking them what they thought of Jonny Bairstow's controversial Ashes stumping and the like.

In truth, it wasn't very difficult at all for me to play this down, because the Australia–England football rivalry is genuinely neither big nor historic. The landscape of football is different from cricket and netball, and women's football is also different from men's football. Men's football – and its traditional powerhouse nations – has been globally established for centuries. The women's game is geographically distinct and largely dictated by the countries who invested early and had national teams available for international fixtures. The US, Brazil and Japan would be more accurate examples of some of our rivalries over the years. Nevertheless, once we were in there, the press pushed, asking about a dozen variations on the same question. It was starting to annoy me after a while, especially when one persistent guy kept pressing the point. I wasn't rude, just kept shutting him down. In the end, I seemed to diffuse the attention when I was asked about all the media attention I was getting. 'I guess the last couple of days have been a pretty big whirlwind for me,' I said in response. 'Obviously, I have not received attention like that before but, at the same time, I just tend to block it out because I know if I play like shit tomorrow it could be a whole different attention on me.' Everyone laughed at that.

I was also asked what I thought about the decision by Nike, the apparel sponsor of both the Australian and English teams, not to produce replica goalkeeper jerseys during the Women's World Cup. Mary Earps, who would be my English counterpart the following night and against whom I played in the WSL whenever West Ham faced Manchester United, had had a crack at Nike before the tournament. 'It is the young kids I am most concerned about,' Earps had said. 'They are going to say, "Mum, Dad, can you get me a Mary Earps shirt?" and they will say, "I can't but I can get you an Alessia Russo 23 or a Rachel Daly 9." What you are saying is that goalkeeping isn't important but you can be a striker if you want.' My comment on the matter, regarding my new personal sponsor, was more diplomatic. 'Obviously, it would be really cool to see kids – or anyone, really – with the goalkeeper jersey on, especially seeing how well goalkeepers have done throughout this whole tournament,' I said. 'In terms of why they don't sell them, I'm not too sure.'

All in all, I thought the press conference went well. I didn't realise at the time that it was quite possibly the biggest of the World Cup so far. I just thought it was normal for 70 or more journalists and camera crew to come to one of these things. When I got back to the hotel, Sam said, 'Holy shit. There were so many people there – that's the biggest one I've seen.' I wouldn't say I enjoyed it, exactly, but it was a good nerve-settler – and I probably won't feel as stressed about doing that sort of thing in the future. Once that was done, I could settle in for the usual match-day-minus-one meal of spaghetti bolognese. The pressure had lifted. We had already exceeded expectations and made the final four for the first time, so that was off our backs.

Sure, we were nervous about the occasion but mostly we were just excited. I had come down from my high, still light but with my feet once again firmly on the ground. That generally happens after my post-match review meeting with Tony F. He didn't have any new or atypical messages. It was basically that the France game was done, so I could tick that off, and now we had to focus on the next one. He always rattles off the same little checklist of bullet points and that was how he started this meeting. Then he took me through a choice few clips. He gassed me up the whole time, telling me how good my performance was and praising me for specific elements. But he mixed that with a few work-ons, saying things like, 'You could still be better on this.' That balance was exactly what I wanted and needed.

It was while I was getting treatment on the morning of the game that I first heard the 'Minister of Defence' nickname. My physio asked if I had seen the video of deputy prime minister Richard Marles handing over his job to me. I hadn't, because I had given up on trying to keep up with social media. I also had absolutely no idea who Richard Marles was or what his joke announcement meant. But from the traction it generated, I figured it must be a pretty big deal. I think I typed and deleted a response to his video three or four times, before coming up with just a couple of emojis. I didn't know how best to respond to the country's actual minister of defence. It was very surreal, though, that the nation had come up with a new nickname for me so soon after barely knowing my first name. For the record, Marles said the following in his stony-faced video, which he posted to X:

> Tonight, our nation faces a grave threat and it comes from the old enemy. And I realise that I am unable to meet the moment, so it is my solemn duty to announce that this afternoon I'm resigning as Australia's minister for defence. And I am handing my commission to Mackenzie Arnold. As Australia expects, I know that in this hour she will do us proud. And I simply ask one thing: tomorrow, can you please give me back the keys?

26.
End of the Road

Kirsty sends me a text before every one of my games, no matter what. She has done this throughout our relationship but during the World Cup she added a little motivation. It was usually along the lines of remembering to be myself and play the way I always do; that she's proud of how far I have come and nobody can take that away from me. She writes each message slightly differently but they all sign off with: 'Good luck my number one, I love you.'

KIRSTY SMITH

I always messaged her before games but because it was early in the morning London time, I'd sometimes write the message the night before and then wake up in the morning, send it, fall back asleep again before the game and then wake up for the game itself. Usually, my messages let her know how proud I was of her and how far she's come, and that this is just the world seeing her for the player she's always been. We always knew what she had in her and it's just amazing everyone else can see it now. When I was in Sydney for the Ireland game, I wore my purple strip she gave me. So every other game after that, I literally went to training in London wearing the strip. I didn't take it off.

I will admit to being a little stressed before the England game. I didn't want to spoil all the hype of the previous four days by allowing us to get slaughtered. Or even just making a mistake that would rip me from this magical place I'd been inhabiting.

I made a solid start by stopping a Georgia Stanway shot with the inside of my right leg. It was a one-on-one with Clare Hunt giving chase. That was the settler. After that, I was good. There's nothing better than ripping off the Band-Aid with a big save early on. There were two key moments for me in this semi-final. One, of course, was Sam's goal. In our sixth game of the tournament, our captain had finally started a match. Ella Toone's opener meant we were trailing 1–0 after the hour mark, chasing an equaliser to keep us in it and needing a magic pill. It's just crazy, the things Sam can do. Conjure something from nothing. She collected the ball inside our half and burst up the field, scared Millie Bright and Jess Carter out of a challenge and let rip from long range. Mary Earps has never had an easy time against Sam – this was her 10th goal against Earps for club and country. Cue 80,000 in delirium and eight minutes of solid-gold hope when we chased a second goal hard, only for Lauren Hemp to spoil the day and Alessia Russo to triple the pain.

We wanted to win so badly but wanting does not always produce the desired effect. This match felt a little different to the last, in that whatever the result, we still felt as if we had achieved something unforgettable. That we had somehow altered the texture of perception. Four years prior, the 2019 World Cup in France was still blighted by blokey blokes who loved to tell anyone willing to listen that women's football was 'too slow' to deserve their time. They might be the same men who spent the 2023 edition dissecting Sam's wonder goal and Mary's perfect pass. Our 3–1 semi-final loss to England was Australia's most-watched television programme, in sport or any other category, since 2001, when the existing rating system was established. Its national reach of 11.15 million surpassed even the 8 million who watched Cathy Freeman win gold at the 2000 Olympics. They are the statistics but it was also everywhere we walked. On the flip side of that, there was still a bit of cheerleading in some sections of women's sport. Well-meaning supporters who viewed performance-related critique as disrespectful because isn't just showing up enough to smash through glass ceilings? This World Cup showed Australia and the world that football – women's and men's – is a sport worthy of time and money because the emotional investment of its supporters has to have somewhere to go. And, conversely, once more, it is never okay for that emotional investment to manifest as sexist, homophobic or other derogatory comments either in person or online. During my pre-match press conference, when I said if I played like shit against England then everything

I had achieved against France would be forgotten, it was a light sugar coating for a pretty serious truth. If I come out to take a cross against England but it slips through my hands and into our goal, that could come to define my World Cup.

The reason I bring this up now is that my hypothetical situation would be no different to if, say, Ellie Carpenter made an error that contributed to one of England's three semi-final goals. When this occurred, it did not seem to matter that Ellie is objectively one of the world's best right-backs, up there with Lucy Bronze and Ona Batlle. She was still roasted online by trolls who knew little about the sport she plays and who did not mention that Ellie converted her penalty against France while I missed mine. Neither of these scenarios are relevant anyway, because sporting teams win together and lose together. I know this, because I have made plenty of errors on the field and because I also have a tendency to search social media for negative comments. Sometimes, it can feel as if someone is always waiting to slam you down. It is why I try to limit what I can see on social media and why I also don't let praise get to my head. In December 2023, FIFA and FIFPRO released data revealing that one in five players experienced online abuse during the 2023 Women's World Cup, with female athletes being 29 per cent more likely to encounter abuse than male players did during the 2022 Men's World Cup finals.

I've definitely been trolled. I think everyone has. All it takes is one bad game or a mistake and you are the worst player in the world – and they are not scared to let you know.

It can be very confusing, because the 'they' is not a tangible group of people you either know or respect. They are people who most likely will never meet or get to know you (some actually aren't even people, but bots), yet for some reason they wield this invisible control over your psyche. If you are outspoken, this is even more the case.

I grew up in the MySpace and MSN era. It was so harmless back then. The worst thing you could do to somebody else was remove them from your top friends list. Growing up, I had such little exposure to social media as we know it today. I have since learned it can be very negative and hostile but that there is also room for people with platforms to do something positive. If I have a bad game, I try to stay off it but I do seem to end up back there a lot of the time. And even if you hate it, celebrity culture demands a social-media presence. The majority of endorsements now are dictated by how many followers you have. Since the World Cup, my DMs have been filled with positive comments. But as much as I adore those, I am prone to seeking out one or two negative comments and focusing on them instead.

I suppose what I am trying to say is: even after we lost that night, we still believed we had done enough and hoped others would believe so, too. And in the end, losing to Sweden in the third-place play-off felt far worse than losing to England and being denied a spot in the final. A spot in the final makes you a finalist and a certain top-two placer. A 2–0 loss in a third-place play-off makes you fourth and nothing more. It was a very similar near-miss to that at the Tokyo Olympics, except at a bigger tournament. After that loss to Sweden back at Suncorp on the tournament's penultimate day, I fully understood what the girls went through at the Olympics. Then you start to struggle with what that means. We had just made history and everybody seemed to be delighted, but history will also show that we came away with nothing tangible around our necks.

The feeling was utter deflation. I don't remember the goals. I don't remember Caitlin getting a black eye. I don't remember anything. After the 90 minutes were over, it felt as if all the air had been let out of the balloon. At the very least, later that evening was a nice time. FA had set up a bar for family and friends so, after we returned to the hotel for dinner, we all went and got dressed and met the people we love to wind down. That was when we were able to celebrate what we had done and feel a little bit of pride. My brother and sister-in-law had to go home because they had the kids, so it was just my mum and dad and uncle and aunty. Shaquille and her boyfriend weren't going to come out at all but I peer-pressured them into it and they ended up booking a hotel for the night. There was also Oli and his wife Phoebe. I knew Oli from way back during my days living in Perth – he designed the Mackenzie 'Brick Wall' Arnold T-shirts that Sam wore on our flight together from London to Perth for our Olympic qualifiers in late 2023.

A lot of us were quite hungover the next morning. I rolled downstairs on about an hour or two of sleep and slumped down next to Alanna at breakfast. She took one look at me and said, 'Come with me.' She took me back to her room and gave me a hat, and told me to wipe my eyes because I had smudged mascara everywhere. Lans was stone-cold sober because her concussion meant she couldn't go anywhere. Her ordering me to sort myself out was pretty funny. Then we all went off to be given the keys to the city by Lord Mayor of Brisbane Adrian Schrinner at a special fan day. Also there was Nikki Webster, who had flown in to surprise us with a personal rendition of 'Strawberry Kisses', thanks to Steph's obsession with the teeny-bopper song. If you look back on footage, you'll notice that a lot of us were wearing sunglasses.

27.
The New Normal

Young boys on bicycles pull up next to our car. They peer into the window for a better look and then take off again. Kirsty and I drive deeper into the caravan park, past cabins and campers and elaborate tent set-ups, on a 10 km/h crawl through the maze to find my parents' camping spot. Lennox Head is a holiday destination from my childhood. The swells here are famous among surfers but not famous enough to draw the main tourist set down from Byron Bay. The promise of this tranquillity over the Christmas and New Year period has kept me going through the back end of 2023, which I have spent in fifth gear just trying to stay abreast of my new life. Nothing could have prepared me for the real-life experience of overnight fame, how the sudden loss of anonymity affects the minutiae of your day-to-day existence. I did anticipate some attention in big Australian cities, such as on our trip to Perth in November to play our first round of Paris Olympics qualifiers. I did not expect to be recognised while grocery shopping at a Tesco in London. Nor did I foresee it at a caravan park in a northern NSW coastal town with a population of fewer than 10,000.

At first, we thought the boys on the bicycles might have just been stickybeaking at all passers-by and thought nothing more of it as we found and greeted my parents at their site. No sooner had we sat down, however, did they return. This time, they pedalled directly towards us. 'Are you Mackenzie Arnold?' one asked. 'Is it really you?' asked another. Every day of our stay, those boys would come for a visit, bringing a football and asking us to play with them. They weren't the only ones, either. Kirsty and I were actually staying at an Airbnb up the road and most days walked the small distance between our accommodation and Mum and Dad's campsite. To get there and back, we had to pass all the caravans and almost every time people would suddenly emerge, seeking confirmation of my identity and then prompting a conversation. In the end, our holiday was filled with these mini-interactions, from the moment we left in the morning until our heads hit the pillow at night.

It was unreal, and bizarre, and wonderful, and exhausting, all at once. You would think you'd get used to it after a while. And maybe I will, in time. But I don't think I will ever feel completely at ease with this sometimes overwhelming new reality. During that same holiday, Kirst and I went with Shaquille to see some Christmas lights on the Gold Coast and strangers were knocking on our car window and mouthing, 'Are you Mackenzie Arnold?' Before, when I came home during the off-season, Shaq and I would go out and run amok, or roll down to the beach for a swim looking like hell, and be completely inconspicuous. Now we can't go to Nando's without three different groups asking me for photos. In the same way that I am awkward with compliments, I think I might be awkward with attention. Photos and autographs are great but sometimes I don't know what to say. What is the correct response when somebody says, 'I love you,' and literally nothing else? What am I supposed to say when I am having a photo with a couple of kids and one shouts out to the woman behind the camera, 'Mum, isn't this the girl you said you'd turn gay for?'

I think my friends would describe me as an extrovert but when I meet new people or am put in a situation I'm not comfortable with, I am far more introverted. These days, I spend most of my time negotiating situations that would typically send me straight back into my shell but I am trying hard to be open and engaging. It is certainly a novel way to move through the world. Fans do seem to feel a closeness to us, as if they know us personally.

Having said all of this, I lean into it as much as I can. I try to be a role model, even though I am as fallible as anyone. An adult still growing up. To be fair, I have done a bit of that over the past few months, since becoming West Ham captain. I was one of the oldest players in our youthful squad and tried to lead in the way I would have appreciated throughout all those years of my own shaky development. I am increasingly competitive and hold myself to much higher standards. I want to win. I want to be that person. I want to start. I want to do everything.

But if someone is better than me, I also know my place and I never forced my mindset onto the rest of the squad. Our manager, Rehanne Skinner, assisted me when I needed it.

In mid-2024, not long before the Paris Olympics and almost exactly four years after joining West Ham, I signed with National Women's Soccer League side Portland Thorns. It was one of the most difficult decisions I have ever had to make. My teammates, coaches and all the staff at Chadwell Heath were so central to helping me become the player I always wanted to be, and giving me confidence when it was lacking. Ultimately, it was time for a new challenge in a new environment, with the added drawcard of working with Jordan Franken again.

Some other people keeping me sane are BK and Mary Smirnis from One Sports & Entertainment. Since the World Cup, I speak to them more than I do my family and most mornings I wake up to a message updating me on various matters, including endorsements and partnerships. They seem to be growing all the time. Whatever it is, they are my sounding board and the filter for the countless enquiries that reach their inboxes. They send me what I need to know and keep it feeling manageable.

Then, there is Kirsty. She is my stability and routine. Every day, that routine begins with an alarm at 9 a.m. – just enough time to get dressed and drive the 15 minutes to our training ground for breakfast at 9:30 a.m. We are usually some of the first in the team to arrive – another Kirsty thing. Before we met, I was one of the last, stretching out every spare minute of sleep I could, until time was no longer on my side. I resisted this new regime at first, though admit I do enjoy not rushing everywhere now. After training, we have lunch with the team and then head into the gym. Then we go home, have a snack and chill out. Sometimes, we watch something on Netflix or catch up on a TV show – usually *Love Island* or *Married at First Sight*. Often, we'll head into London for dinner or eat something easy with friends. If we're at home, it's HelloFresh, which basically stops us from cooking the same thing over and over. We both do a bit of everything but Kirsty takes more control with making the sauces and dressings, because I get scared I'll stuff that part up. I wouldn't say I have a specialty but Kirsty loves my fajitas, so I do them sometimes to give her a night out of the kitchen. Kirsty has heaps of dishes but my favourite is her match-day-minus-one pasta dish. It's called marry-me pasta and is full of sundried tomatoes, chicken, cream and some other things. It's the bomb. Then we're into bed with *Gogglebox* on in the background with a sleep timer and are usually sound asleep by 11 p.m.

These are my controllables. They are the solid foundations of a life lived in the clouds, to where I retreat when unreality hits. I got another dose in February 2024, during our final Olympic qualifier. When we bought our ticket to Paris with a 10–0 victory over Uzbekistan, the green and gold of Marvel Stadium's stands was speckled with purple. I had kept pretty quiet about Nike's decision to not sell goalkeeper jerseys during the World Cup, being new on their books and reluctant to ruffle feathers. In the end, I didn't need to say anything. As goalkeepers made names for themselves all over the world, passionate fans applied the pressure and Nike finally responded to the demand. A couple of days before our home leg against Uzbekistan, the brand announced it would start printing my purple goalkeeper shirt. It sold out in minutes. On the way to the game, I looked out the window to see three purple jerseys running next to our team bus. Running alongside them were a couple of Kerr and Foord jerseys. I do belong here, after all.

Powered by Penguin

Looking for more great reads, exclusive content and book giveaways?

Subscribe to our weekly newsletter.

Scan the QR code or visit penguin.com.au/signup